"The ten transformational miracle~ ~~
book, including his own, were all ~
think they will inspire ALL who re

Dane Anderson
President and Chief Executive Officer
FAST Global Solutions, Inc., Minnesota

"Rick Mattson has written a book about struggling people who
have an authentic and sometimes messy encounter with a
delightful and disturbing and wooing God. Whatever your faith
background or orientation, you will be inspired and encouraged
by these real life and powerful stories!"

Dr. Rick Richardson, Professor of Intercultural Studies
Wheaton College and the Billy Graham Center
Author: *Experiencing Healing Prayer* and *The Heart of Racial Justice*

"The ten people in this book are offering us a gift. They have
invited us to a 'pause-point' saying, basically, 'Hey! Take a break!
Slow down, give me your attention, and let me share with you
something remarkable, something that you might want, and
something that you can have!' I think the reader will find it hard
to put this book down, and will be compelled to share the stories
with others."

Dr. Michael Hein, M.D., Healthcare CEO
Grand Island, Nebraska

Faith Unexpected:

Real Stories of People Who Found What They Never Imagined

Rick Mattson

Cover design: Dan Clayton

Interior design: Ryan and Maggie Mattson

ISBN soft cover 978-0-692-04899-3
ISBN ebook 978-0-9997740-0-7
Pavement Publishing

Author's ministry website: www.rickmattsonoutreach.com

Faith Unexpected **book website** and order form:
www.faithunexpectedstories.com

Bulk discounts available for churches.
Email us at mattsonoutreach@gmail.com for information.

Acknowledgements

I wish to thank each of the persons I interviewed for this book: Charles, James, Sarah, Deedra, Cole, Una, York, Donald, and Nicole. You were willing to share your stories in order to encourage and inspire others. Thank you so much!

To my editorial team of Sharon Sheppard, Sharon Aaseng, Sharon Mattson and Sarah (not Sharon) Kane – I appreciate your sharp eyes and many suggestions.

Contents

Introduction

Stories shape our lives. And our lives are, in themselves, stories. Part of my own story took shape in a class called "Advanced Creative Writing," at Southwest Minnesota State University. One day our professor did a five-minute reading from a book that changed me forever – a reading *not* from Shakespeare or Dickenson or Chaucer, but from Hamilton. You know, *Donald* Hamilton?

Probably doesn't ring a bell.

The book is called *Death of a Citizen*, and its main character, Matt Helm, is a civilian who's forced to work in counter-intelligence for a secret government agency during the Cold War.

After narrating a few pages to our class, the professor held the paperback novel over his head and declared to fifteen wannabe authors, "Now *that's* good writing."

Wow, I never saw that coming. A professor I really respected had just given me permission . . . no, more than that, had just given me *inspiration* to read further in my favorite genre.

I went on to devour all twenty-seven books in the Matt Helm series, and even began to think of myself as a budding writer. That was more than thirty-five years ago.

This book

The stories contained in the book you're holding are meant to inspire something in you. The subject matter is not international espionage or secret agents, but something even more mysterious: faith.

In the current spiritual climate of skepticism in America, I find it astonishing that anyone at all would find faith. Most of the characters in these pages, all of whom are real people, pretty much stumbled into their faith in God. They never expected it, weren't looking for it; some didn't even think it was possible.

I can't wait for you to read about Sarah Gross, who fought *against* faith at a liberal private college, or York Moore who was a suicidal skeptic, or Deedra Reyess who was enmeshed in the dark world of spirits on a Native American reservation in Arizona. And then there is Donald Wellington whose military career and work at the Pentagon does, in fact, remind me of the "Matt Helm" universe. His story is told in chapter eight, and perhaps when you read it you'll feel the same sense of mystique about Mr. Wellington that I felt when I interviewed him in Washington, D.C.

You

It's quite possible that you've got a bit of faith going in your life these days. Faith in God, I mean. It's rather out of vogue, currently, but to my thinking that's what makes faith more attractive. Who wants to just run with the crowd? That's the easy way out.

In fact, I maintain that there's a deep sense of intrigue at the spiritual level of life, and that many of us really do desire a "faith-walk," if only we knew where to look or what to read or who to ask.

It's also quite possible you don't have any faith in God at all. That's totally okay. There will be several stories like yours of folks who never even knew about faith, or who tasted something bitter (or simply unconvincing) among believers and left it behind for greener pastures. Later, they returned for a fresh start, and maybe you will too, I don't know.

Regardless of your current state of mind, I hope you'll be inspired by these stories. They represent ordinary persons from around the country who are diverse in age – from twenty to near seventy – and

2

ethnicity – including Black, Asian, Latino, Native American, and White. They all told me powerful accounts of finding faith . . . faith that was, in every single case, *unexpected.*

Notes

- On page 110 you'll find a Reflection Guide to help you think through and respond to what you're reading. The guide also works as a basis for discussion with a friend about the book.

- On page 112 there are instructions for how to formalize your faith, if you wish. For some readers that may be too much of a leap forward for now. For others, they just want very specific instructions, point by point, on how to nail down something they (perhaps) never imagined for themselves.

P.S. I hope you make it to the final chapter and read my own story, "Rick Mattson: Lost Rocker," so you can learn what it was that took me by surprise and eventually captured my heart.

- 1 -

Charles Ramirez: Macho Man

Phoenix

Young Charles Ramirez had his eye on a girl named Jane, best friend of his sister. Unfortunately, he was stationed three hundred miles away at Nellis Air Force Base in Las Vegas. But upon returning home to Phoenix on leave, he landed a couple dates with the cute girl, and much to his satisfaction, the relationship took flight and progressed quickly over a period of months.

As they grew closer and began talking dreamily about sharing a house and family someday, Jane uttered a certain sentence that would, going forward, determine the direction of their lives, for better or worse. It was a prophetic statement but also quite naive on her part:

"Charles, we are destined to be together *forever.*"

Forever was a long time, thought Charles. But he wasn't put off by the idea. On the contrary, he could see "together forever" working to his advantage, since he interpreted the phrase much differently than did Jane – she envisioning two blissful love-birds entwined in each other's lives, inseparably, for all time.

But in *his* mind, such permanence offered the best of two worlds: his girlfriend would be fenced in securely by her commitment to him and a family, and he as the man of the house would be free to indulge his many pleasures. A winning combination.

He'd developed a robust appetite for booze, weed, cocaine and meth while serving in the Air Force. So when the couple got together in 1979, it wasn't long before Charles turned a wandering eye to enticements outside the nest.

With Jane anchored at home and caring for little kids, Charles plunged lustily into the alluring nightlife of Phoenix. In so doing, he was following the footsteps of his father and uncles before him, what Charles calls the "macho man" way of ruling a home.

"My dad and his brothers were always drinking, always partying, the man of the house doing whatever he wanted, whenever he wanted – as long as he met one condition: he had to provide for his family, had to make sure they were taken care of. After that, anything goes.

"Jane and the kids said I was selfish, leaving them at home, but I never saw it because I always thought, 'I'll give you whatever you want.' The kids always had the best toys, the best baseball gear. There was food on the table . . . so fine, Dad can do whatever he pleases."

Committed to Jane by day but single by night, Charles caroused the town with other women, drank beer and took drugs, often staying out into the wee hours of morning. Yet, every day he went to his job as an electronic technician, earned a solid paycheck, paid the bills.

In this lifestyle, however, trouble was inevitable.

The altercation

One night Charles was in a bar with two of his drinking buddies, including a cousin who got into a fight with an on-duty bouncer. The conflict escalated as the two combatants lurched violently into the men's room, where the cousin pulled a pocket knife on the bouncer and cut him up, then fled the scene. That left Charles and his brother-in-law, Rudy, at the bar, drinking and playing pool. They

5

reasoned, *Hey, we didn't do anything wrong. Not our fight. Let's finish our beers and complete this game,* which they did. Finally departing, they stopped at a liquor store on the way home to buy more beer, when out of nowhere a swarm of police converged on their vehicle.

Charles and Rudy were taken to the hospital where the bouncer was being treated for his wounds. On seeing the two guys he nearly jumped out of bed, pointing at Jane's man. "Yeah! That's him! He's the one who did it!"

The boys were hauled off to jail to be prosecuted, Charles for assault with a deadly weapon. He spent ten days behind bars and was rescued only because a judge with common sense pressed the bulky six-foot-five-inch bouncer on whether Charles, at five-seven, one-sixty, had actually forcibly moved him into a restroom brawl. The truth came out and Charles was able to return to work.

But nothing changed. There was no moral to the story for Charles, no lesson to be learned from the harsh confines of jail. Released, the party animal simply went back on the prowl, into the night, his appetites ever insatiable, his judgments . . . highly questionable.

The stickup

He tells of an evening cruising the streets of Phoenix, alone in his vehicle, when he pulled alongside some attractive young pedestrian traffic to ask about any good parties that might be in the area. Two ladies and a guy boarded the car and steered their chauffeur through a series of meaningless turns toward a non-existent "rager" of strong drink and cocaine, when Charles felt the tip of a gun pressed against his neck.

No physical harm occurred but Charles lost his wallet and something of his emotional well-being. He was traumatized by the armed robbery and required the services of a counselor.

Faithful Jane, as usual, had been home by herself with the kids.

Reaction from home

Eventually the couple got married, but it didn't stop Jane from taking action against her wayward provider. Charles remembers, "When my daughter was six years old, I walked into the house one morning from partying all night, and my wife had my bags packed, sitting by the door. She said, 'I don't want you here anymore. You're out.'

"But my daughter picked up the bags and took them to her room. She said, 'Dad is staying with me.'

"Another time, when my son was in seventh grade, Jane was fed up with me again, so she kicked me out, and I moved in with my brother who lived in the same housing complex just two buildings over. A couple days later Jane walked over and said to me, 'Come back. I can't see your son moping around sad, because he misses you.'"

Charles cannot relate these stories without choking on the words. Yet, as he reflects now, his after-hours collisions with various shady characters and the police, and the brief separations from his wife "did nothing to open my eyes. I was still blind to my own selfish ways."

A day of reckoning was looming, however, a judgment to be handed out against him. The self-entitled "man of the house" was soon to be forced out of the fast lane into a gut-punching, heart-smashing, life-sucking, dreadful, horrible . . . lonely . . . dead end.

7

Hitting the wall

It all began in the usual way, Jane tossing him out of the house – again. Probably not a problem, long term. She'd come around. She'd realize her need for him, just like always. It might take a few days or a week or two, but Charles was confident his banishment would be temporary. If nothing else, the kids would protest such harsh treatment and step in to revoke his sentence.

Only this time, things were different. The kids stepped in all right, but in precisely the opposite way of the past.

Charles can hardly tell the story now, his words buried in emotion. "We had a big argument . . . It was on a Sunday morning . . . the fighting. I'll never forget it [long pause]. My son actually threw a punch at me. My own son! It wasn't meant to hit me, because he held back. . . But that's how much anger was in him . . . I could see the rage and the hate [Charles crying now] . . . My son was my best friend. Despite all my bad ways, we did everything together. I coached him for years. One lady had even said to me when I was kicked out of the house, 'Where's your son? He's always with you.' That's the greatest compliment a dad could hear. But now it was over.

"I left the house that Sunday morning and didn't have anywhere to go. Eventually I got my own apartment, in exchange for working there. The separation lasted a long while, and those were the loneliest years of my life. There were times where I didn't even sleep on the bed. I didn't want to go to bed because there was nothing there.

"All the times I was with my wife, I thought of myself as a single man. But now I was truly a single man. I tried to go out, tried to do things I'd done before, tried to go back to what I wanted or thought I wanted to do, but it just wasn't happening. Nothing there."

Something new

Christians at his place of work had encouraged him in the past to go to church, which he resisted. He'd grown up around the church but, "It really didn't connect with me. I did all the things you're supposed to do – baptism, communion – all the things a religious person would do. But no one in the family really got involved. It's something we did on Christmas and Easter."

He started attending church with a co-worker, an environment that felt strange for a few weeks, but he kept at it.

Soon he was reading the Bible, discovering within himself a seed of faith, taking an interest in the life of Jesus. Hope was germinating. Still, the loneliness of the solo apartment was lethal to his communal heart, a people-person denied the connection he craved.

"Sometimes I would go a whole week without any physical human contact. People at church would shake my hand and give me a hug, but then nothing for seven days. It was so painful.

"There were nights I wouldn't say anything – from when I left work till the next morning, I wouldn't talk. Not opening your mouth, not touching anyone for a week . . . I was miserable, so lonely. That's the hurt I don't want anyone else to go through. That's why I want to tell my story. The pain was just overwhelming. I couldn't sleep at night; I just lay there."

Epiphany

Then it happened. The inexplicable. The Sistine Chapel moment came like a thunderbolt to the hurting soul. He never saw it coming, nor can he explain it in purely rational terms: a mystical encounter with God.

Back in the sixteenth century, Michelangelo, in his famous painting on the Sistine's ceiling, depicted God reaching out to touch the first man, *Adam*. Charles can relate. "One night I was crying in bed, and I said to God, 'What do you want from me? What do you want?' And I felt this hand on my back. I turned around to see what it was and there was nothing there. I thought it was a pillow. But I was holding my only pillow, crying into it. I still felt this hand on my back. That's when I knew, Jesus is for real. He wanted me."

Adam became a "living being" as a result of God's personal touch. But what of Charles? Would the hand of God make any difference to him? Would he too come *alive*?

The yard in the middle

Odds were against. His basic outlook went all the way back to central Phoenix, to age seven when his mom abandoned the family to pursue a perverse lover – chemicals. He and his siblings were then raised in a single-parent home called the "back house," which was separated from the property's "front house" by a large lawn.

Grandmother and two aunts lived in the front house, and the big yard in-between became the scene of a continuous party where strong drink flowed in abundance for decades. Here, kids played games and sports innocently enough, but also hustled beverages for grownups, skimming mouthfuls of beer as a tip for courier services rendered.

"They didn't have drugs back then, but the men drank constantly. It was a way of life. Still, credit my dad – he always supported us. He gave Grandma the money to buy food and take care of us. She and my two aunts were our mother figures, while we played baseball and football outdoors."

The family's real mother, of course, was absent. Her storyline will always have a beginning and ending for Charles, but no middle. Nothing in the middle except the aching silence of abandonment. She died of alcohol poisoning in 1984. "When we arrived at the hospital she was already unconscious. I hadn't seen her since I was seven years old." [Charles weeps]

Would a man born into the bottle, raised on the bottle, his mom drowned in a bottle, be able to shake himself loose from the bottle – the liquid devil – even if he'd been touched by God?

Fire

For Charles, the hand of God seemed to penetrate skin, organs and bones, igniting his soul into robust flame. "When God touched me, that's when I completely decided, well, I was just on fire. I turned my dining area into a study, shut off the TV and started concentrating on the Bible. I didn't want to go back to my old life or be that man again."

Reading the Scriptures and participating in a faith community began to pry open stubborn eyes to an alarming revelation: "When I became a Christian and my eyes opened up, I knew that Jesus forgave me. He died for my sins *but I couldn't forgive myself.* That was the hardest thing.

"All those times I was out doing the wrong thing, thinking, who's going to find out? Does it matter to anybody? But slowly I was killing my family. I think about all the laughter I took from my kids and my wife, all the things that I stole from them by being absent as a husband and father. They're never going to get that back."

With God in his life, Charles was seeing the world open afresh before him, loaded with possibilities for healing and restoration. Yet, he still felt alone at sea. He wanted his family back. "I missed my son. I really, really missed my best friend, the guy that I was always with. I needed them all back."

The thaw

During the separation, Jane and Charles began meeting up on a park bench in the housing complex where she still lived. He told her he'd been attending church and was excited about finding faith in Jesus and changing his life with God's help. She took this news skeptically, like a thirsty desert traveler, another mirage of water on the horizon sure to disappoint.

"It's just another one of your things," she said, eyes rolling. "You went to AA already, pledged to change. Every few years you go through a cycle of reform, but nothing ever comes of it. This is the same thing all over again, an empty promise."

But over time she saw a new consistency in Charles – substantive change from party-guy to a decent, stay-at-home man. He read the Bible, attended church, cared about people – especially her.

She gave him another chance.

Another chance, yes, but with more than a shade of doubt in her heart. *If he screws up this time . . .*

Marked man

Meanwhile, Charles was seeing troubled people in his community with fresh eyes. He remembers his chance encounter with a boozer: "I was walking down the street going to the grocery store one day, and there was a drunk sitting on a bench, and he said, 'Hey, come and tell me about that cross on your shoulder.'"

This was in reference to the symbol of a cross and the words "Galatians 2:20" (a Bible verse about living for Christ) tattooed onto his upper right arm.

"So I sat there with him for about twenty minutes talking about it. He said, 'I have a pastor's phone number in my wallet, and I'm going to call it. I made good money but I lost my job and I'm losing my family because of my drinking.'

"So I told him, 'You've been carrying that phone number around for a reason. God wants you to call the pastor and talk with him.' And the guy said, 'I will. But before you go, would you give me a hug? I know I smell, I stink, and I'm drunk. But *please* . . . give me a hug.' So I gave him a big bear hug. And that's the reason why I wear this tattoo, as a reminder for me, and to show everyone else what God can do to change a life."

Passages

Jane finally came to Passages Christian Fellowship with her husband, and was startled by the teaching she heard. "What did you tell that pastor about me?" she pressed Charles. "He's talking about me . . . actually, *to* me. He knows way too much about me."

"Nothing!" Charles laughed. "Honey, that's how it was when I first came here too. Pastor Keith seemed to be speaking right into my life. I don't know how he does it."

Soon after, the kids and grandkids heard all the excitement about Passages, and now Charles smiles when he talks about his whole family coming to church together. "All our lives are changing from what they used to be; it's so exciting." And he and his son are talking again, hanging out.

Indeed, one day when I visited the church all the way from my home in Minnesota, there was Charles and his many relatives – including his father, worshiping together in a long row. Charles had a big grin on his face most of the service, mingled with tears of wonder and satisfaction.

Parting words

"The things God took away from me, I never want them back. I never want the drugs, the alcohol, the fooling around, being with other women. I want God, family and church. Those are the three things I want.

"And I remember that time four decades ago when Jane said we would be together forever – and we will be now, now that we both have God in our hearts. And. . . it's amazing what he can do."

- 2 -

James Chambers: On Mission

Inglewood, California

Astrange rustling noise near the back door is eerily out of place, even amid the scratchy creaks and groans of the cheap apartment off Crenshaw Boulevard. Fourteen-year-old James Chambers awakens uneasily, pulling the covers over his head for protection, listening intently. Ten seconds of silence, then the little clamor comes again to his ears, source unknown, most likely bad guys though. A paralysis of fear creeps into his legs and shoulders and lower back, his mind searching frantically for options.

He keeps a baseball bat handy, precisely for this situation, leaning against his bed. But with his body frozen in terror, would he be able to grab it, swing it, fight for his life? His mind jumps over to a second option, another line of defense – a handgun stashed in a cabinet drawer in the other room, to be used only, *only* in dire emergency, his father had warned. Too bad Dad is working overnight, leaving the kid and his sister home alone in not the best of neighborhoods.

The boy weighs the risks. If he could possibly get to the gun before contact with the enemy, he'd stand a fighting chance. But that would mean getting out of bed, sneaking into the living room and loading the clip, probably too late. He's too scared to move anyway. No, he would simply have to accept his fate, a life of just fourteen years ending tonight.

15

The rattling from the back door continues intermittently, attacking his senses, each vibration a little spike run into his gut. His mind looks ahead to the inevitable, to death, to the moment of passing from this life to the next, what it will feel like . . . suddenly a further realization crashes his brain, throwing him deeper into hellish terror: within a few minutes he will be coming into direct contact with God Almighty!

James screams silently, overcome with anguish, feeling helpless against both God and man. He cannot face his Maker now, not without preparation, not without being *baptized*. The preacher said you had to be baptized. But the boy had never done it, never taken the opportunity, and now his life was ending prematurely, but he wasn't ready to meet God, hadn't followed all the right steps.

Twenty years later, a grown man reflects back on that panicky night. "I'm thinking it's over for me, but where am I about to go? Heaven? Hell? I'm not that bad of a dude. I've never killed anybody. I help old ladies cross the street. But there are also things that I *don't* do. And I know God knows about them, and if he looks at those things, I'm screwed."

An idea occurs to the unbaptized kid lying in bed. He is desperate, and since his chances against an intruder are slim, he decides to focus on the bigger picture, something within his power: Why not simply get ready for God? The glass of water on his nightstand – that's it! He always gets thirsty at night but doesn't care to walk to the bathroom for a drink, so he fills the glass with water before bedtime . . .

Another ominous patter near the back door, perhaps shoes standing on the porch, eyes peering into a window, or maybe a criminal in the house already. James must act, force his body to function. He shoves his right arm outside the covers, grabs hold of

16

the glass of water, and with a short prayer of, "God, here goes. I hope this works," dumps the cold liquid on his head in holy baptism, *self-baptism.*

Water runs down his face and soaks the pillow underneath.

The creepy noises stop. For a long time, nothing, silence except the normal background groans of an aging building. He gains composure, begins to think rationally, gets up to have a look around, wondering maybe if being half-asleep/half-awake had something to do with the horror movie just played. He checks the back door and it's still locked, no one around except himself and his younger sister who's still asleep. He returns to his room and finds peaceful slumber the remainder of the night. In a damp bed.

Youth ministry

An hour from Brentwood School, the fine college prep institution James attended, is West Angeles Church of God in Christ, a big church with a thriving youth ministry, and through the invitation of some kids there, James joined in, now as a "baptized" believer.

"I experienced something new at the church," he recounts. "In L.A., it's all about how you look, the persona, who you're cliqued up with or not. But here I experienced sincere love from forty teenagers who cared about each other. It was nothing like outside in the streets of Inglewood."

Yet, he didn't understand the worship or what everyone was really talking about regarding God. "My understanding, or *mis*understanding of God was just one thing – morality: Stop bad behavior, start good behavior, that was about it."

Chicago

Following high school, James moved halfway across the country to enroll in Lake Forest College, just north of Chicago, mainly to play basketball, but he was miserable soon after arrival. Basketball was rough that first year, and he realized he'd gone from "sunny L.A. to a place in the Midwest where it gets down to minus-twenty degrees. I didn't know that was possible."

He continued a lifestyle that began back in California when he'd been only seventeen, attaining "VIP" status in the nightclubs up and down Sunset Strip. Here in Chicago, he and friends met up with some Bears football players and soon he was in the VIP lounges of his new city as well, a way to cope with being away from home.

Depressed and on the verge of leaving Lake Forest that first year, he received an invitation to attend a Bible study. "I wasn't so far gone that it was weird. It still interested me. I'd never read the Bible before and didn't really know God. But I was also thinking in my heart, I've got this other thing going in the clubs . . . "

His loyalties thus divided, the athlete-party guy decided to do *both*, so he showed up to the Bible study but also kept on clubbing. Looking back, laughing, he remembers, "I went to this awkward group. I'm the only black guy there, the only inner city guy. It was me and these intellectual suburban white women, basically, and a couple other guys sometimes – definitely a cross-cultural experience. But I was beginning to find some kind of faith."

The prophecy

The following summer James was home in L.A., training for basketball and returning to his roots in the church. One of the leaders there told him that he, James, would soon be "sharing Jesus" with all his friends and everyone he meets.

Of this little prophecy, James was skeptical, especially considering his divided loyalties between church and the clubs. Soon after, however, the leader's words were put to the test.

Crystal

James and two friends were out for an evening, over near LAX, when they met a girl outside Rally's restaurant. Her name was Crystal, and she was in trouble.

As James tells it now: "Crystal's being pimped and had been abandoned for the night, so she asks us if she can borrow a cell phone. The three of us guys are athletes in college and we're starting to act like Christians, but it's still a struggle. We hadn't figured out how to respect women with all the partying going on. If God was mad at us for something, it was in the women department, for sure. We didn't do a great job honoring the ladies.

"Now here is this girl standing in front of us with hardly any clothes on, heels this high, chest hanging out, skirt up to here . . . so my boy Jerod, he hands her his cell phone while looking away like this [James looking away]."

They realize Crystal is in trouble, so they invite her to have dinner with them at Rally's, which turns into an hours-long conversation. "She tells us her mom kicked her out of the house, and one of her teachers told her she was too stupid to be in school, so she dropped out. Until that moment we thought maybe she was twenty-two, twenty-three, and in college. But it turns out she was only sixteen. When we heard that, everything in us just drops."

James starts talking with her about God, but he doesn't know how to say anything. He finally thinks of an approach, so he ventures out, "Crystal, look up at me. Do you know that God loves you?"

The girl is confused. No one has really loved her before, she insists, certainly not God. James the new Jesus-sharer feels deep compassion for her and admits, "I'm kind of new to this God thing myself and I don't know a whole lot about it. But here's what I do know," and he shares his transformation story, such as it is thus far.

As she listens to James and the various tainted stories of her new companions, Crystal begins to melt, identifying profoundly with what they're saying. "You guys actually sound a lot like me," she observes. You came out of some bad stuff."

"Well, we ain't too special," James replies.

She pauses and thinks. "Do you think God will love me like he loves you all?"

"Man, that's exactly what we've been trying to tell you for three hours!" James is adamant. "But we're not too good at it. We don't have any experience. But yeah, he loves you just the same as us."

Crystal places her faith in Jesus that night, and James recalls that her eyes, which were so grim and dark before, were filled with light. "Yeah, she had a busted grill . . . her mouth was all messed up. But then she got this big old smile on her face, totally unashamed, and she said 'I'm so happy, so happy for the first time.' And she's crying . . . "

The encounter had a profound effect on James as well. "I realized that God was on a mission and that I was part of his team. His kingdom was all about making everyone who is broken whole again. And, that God could use me, a totally jacked up dude, at age nineteen, for his work. It totally changed me. I got addicted to helping other people find God's love."

Seeing is believing

A few years ago, before James ever told me his whole story, I was with him at a weekend conference at a hotel in Chicago. By then he was in a ministry to college students full-time. He'd brought a prayer team to the conference from his local church, and they were praying during the lunch hour that God would display his power to the students gathered.

The afternoon session took everyone by surprise as James led a service where a dozen students came forward and received healing for various ailments. One student couldn't put any pressure on his right leg, and after prayer was hopping up and down on it with no pain, for which we all thanked God.

I remember David, sitting next to me in the final session – David the atheist, from the University of Illinois at Chicago. He said he would never believe in Jesus, and so, ironically, James called him forward to witness a healing firsthand. David walked to the front a bit defiantly, sitting next to James as the team prayed for a young woman's leg, that it would grow out to its full length.

Of course, these things can be deceiving. A short leg appears to grow but it's just the energy of the moment, or the wishful thinking of the patient, or the demanding manner of the "faith healer." It seems to me none of these conditions were present, that in fact this limping student needed a full-length limb, and that through humble prayer her leg grew out that evening, maybe an inch, to its complete extension. In any case, the most skeptical person in the room saw it happen up close, and he came back to me visibly moved. "Well?" I asked simply.

"I just saw a healing," David replied, shaking his head. "I can't deny it. It really happened." Later that evening he gave his life to

Jesus, and joined the Christian fellowship at his school. Just another normal day in the life of James Chambers.

Dude to dude

Now it's 2016, and James is telling me his full story of coming to faith, including a remarkable encounter with a nasty dude:

James and a friend run into four of the "Latin Kings" – a famous gang in Chicagoland – on the beach at Lake Michigan. They talk with the gang members about God, and one named Carl shows some interest. But the conversation is cut short when the gang exits the beach quite suddenly.

Skip ahead two months, James praying in his sun-porch early on a Sunday morning as he always does, asking God who he might invite to church that day. "I hear the Holy Spirit saying to my heart, 'Go down Tenth Street,' but it's two hours before church, so I wasn't sure what to do.

"Anyway, I get in my car, flip-flops on, backwards hat, basketball shorts, and I just go out. This is about eight-thirty in the morning, and I'm driving down Tenth Street, and guess who I see walking down the road toward me? Carl. Right there, it's Carl."

James pulls over and approaches the Latin King. "Hey Carl, do you remember me?"

He cocks his head and looks at James. "Yeah, actually. You're that Bible dude from the beach, right?"

"That's me. Last time we got interrupted because your boys had to go. But do you have a couple minutes? Cause I'd like to be real straight and blunt with you."

"Yeah, go ahead, I ain't doing nothing. It's eight-thirty in the morning, man."

"This is what I see," James starts in. "You are in a prison . . . Even though you're in a gang, you are not like your other gang member friends. You're not like your boys. What I'm saying to you, does that make sense?"

"Yeah man, that makes a lot of sense. A year and a half ago, my girl got pregnant, and then she had a miscarriage. I got so pissed off, so angry, I looked for a way to carry out my rage, and it was through the gang."

James notes in his recollection of the story that Carl was what's known as the *enforcer* of the gang. He was the guy you called in to handle different "situations," and was very good at his job.

Carl continues, "You talk about a prison, that's what I feel like on the inside – I feel trapped in a prison and I can't get out."

"Carl, I'm just being very straight with you. Jesus is somebody who came not just to get you to heaven and miss hell, but to set you free from all the things that hold you down, all the things you've done wrong to other people, the way you destroyed your family and neighborhood. He wants to come in and set you free from that addictive behavior of anger, so you can be free to love."

Carl is drawn in. "Man, that sounds good. I've never heard this before. How do I do it?"

A few minutes later Carl is riding home with James to meet his wife and son, and they all enjoy a big breakfast together before heading off to church, Carl in his black hoodie from the night before, "baggie jeans hanging down to here," as James tells it, "smelling like a party. He's never been to church before. He's just how he is, living his life."

They go to the altar during the worship time and Carl gives his life to God. Two weeks later James begins meeting with him, teaching him what it means to follow Jesus. He tells Carl this new

23

relationship is just like knowing another person. You get to know their character and desires so well, you can almost predict what they're going to do. That's how it is in knowing God personally.

The new father

After Carl's conversion experience at church, he and James began praying together regularly, and Carl came to a profound realization: "James, I think God is showing me something about my niece and nephew. Their dad left them, and their mom – my sister – is stuck over the border in Mexico and can't get back because of immigration issues. So they're stuck here in America, and my mom (their grandma), takes care of them. And I think God may want me to be a father them, to really take care of them."

"Wow, you look very emotional," James replied, "like you want to cry or something. Is there anything else you'd like to share?"

"Dude, I didn't tell you this, but the tattoos on my arm are *osito*, which is Spanish for 'little bear.' And when my girl lost our boy, I called him my osito, my little bear. And I felt like God just gave me Little Bear back. He just gave me two kids to take care of, to be a father to, for when I lost my son, lost my boy. And I'm emotional because I feel like God really knows me. And now I'm knowing him. I never saw this coming."

The traveling minister

These days, James travels the country speaking to churches about how they can better reach out to their communities with the message of Jesus Christ.

You can find him at www.afaiththatoverflows.com

- 3 -

The Wooing of Sarah Gross

San Francisco

When Sarah was eight years old, her father told her that she was capable of becoming president of the United States, and he insisted that being female *in no way* disqualified her from that position. He sat her down on a stool in their living room, in front of a pretend microphone, and interviewed her as if she'd already risen to the Oval Office:

"Madam President," he said, "what will you do about poverty? Racism? What will you do if the Soviet Union declares war?"

The girl was already literate in the issues of the day. She had to be in order to participate in the nightly debates around the family dinner table, where politics and religion were hashed out, often heatedly.

"My dad, he treated me like an equal," she says now. "He and my mom and my six older sisters helped shape me into a progressive, thinking woman."

Macalester

Ten years later, the progressive, thinking woman enrolled at Macalester College in St. Paul, Minnesota, arriving on campus in a kind of double mood. She was feeling compassion for the hurting and marginalized of society but also fierce anger toward religion, especially Christianity. Of this latter mood, she remembers that it wasn't hard to find partners at Macalester. "My friends and I

25

believed that organized religion was the main cause of most of the ills of society, including racism, homophobia, and sexism," she recalls.

So they took action – ripping down posters belonging to the Christian club on campus, and during late night sessions in the dorms, arguing fiercely with their opponents. "I remember this one student from Illinois," she says now. "She grew up in the church and had very warm feelings toward her background and family. We debated her aggressively until she cried. To this day I regret that we tore down what was so meaningful to her."

Acting against religion, however, didn't prevent the young West Coast liberal from acting *for* causes she believed in, such as equality. So when she heard about a march for women's rights that was soon to occur in Washington, D.C., she boarded a bus filled with Macalester students and traveled to the nation's capital to join the event, spring of her freshman year. There she marched in solidarity with thousands of other demonstrators in and around the monuments and memorials of the expansive National Mall.

Then it happened. Totally unexpected. It took her by surprise: counter-protesters. She didn't understand what was going on. Who could be against women's rights? They approached her, shrieking insanely. They thrust a jar containing a fetus – an animal fetus – into her face, forcing her to look at it, screaming their pro-life creed. She ran away, horrified.

It was a severely disturbing incident for Sarah. On the long ride back to Minnesota, she found herself hardening even more toward organized religion in all its ugly forms. And she well remembered her parents' instruction to *always* question authority and *always* stand against oppression. Certainly the pro-life extremists were both, and she resolved to oppose them.

Back on campus, her increasing antipathy was reinforced by professors in her classes. "Many of them were the same as me: down on God and the church," she says now. "They had scholarly credentials, and it was just implied in class that if you disagreed with them and believed in religion, you were probably an idiot."

Hearing from beyond

Sarah wore what she calls an "angry face" in those days, especially around anything to do with belief in a higher power. Yet, in quiet moments, away from the rigors of studies and activism, she felt a growing desire – an *ache*, she calls it now – for some kind of spirituality in her life. But she didn't know what that meant. How could you be spiritual . . . but avoid religion or a higher power? She had no answer.

She met Megan in the dorms. "Beautiful woman, brown hair," she remembers now. "Megan had an ethereal quality about her that drew me in. She told me she had recently visited a 'spirit channeler' who helped her connect with spirits that spoke into her life and provided guidance. I was immediately excited and intrigued by all this, and wanted to experience it for myself, but I was also a little afraid."

Megan agreed to go along with Sarah on her spiritual quest to the neighboring city of Minneapolis. There they entered a lovely hundred-year-old home of hardwood floors, muted rugs and tapestries, and discreet lamps that emitted soft halos of light, giving the rooms of the house a subdued glow.

"Deborah" welcomed them warmly, and after brief introductions, turned on a tape recorder and fell into a trance.

"I was mesmerized," Sarah recalls. "Deborah became a conduit for spirits that were speaking to me about my past. They were naming things that had happened in my childhood, and they told about other spirits from prior generations of my family. Also, there was a stream of utterances regarding the direction of my future."

After the session, Deborah provided a detailed analysis of everything on the tape, and Sarah listened to the recording over and again in the weeks to follow. A gap in her life was being filled, she thought: a curtain drawn open to a realm of both mystery and revelation. That was the paradox. It was here that she sought guidance for career, major at school, choice of boyfriend, insight into family past and present . . . and reassurance that she was okay.

The R.A.

The position of Resident Advisor (R.A.) in dormitories is a sought-after appointment on most college campuses, carrying with it not only leadership opportunities (and resume points), but financial incentives as well. Sarah applied for the R.A. slot in Wallace Hall, third floor, her junior year at Macalester, and got it.

One last fling, however, before school began in the fall: a two-week backpacking trek on the Pacific Crest Trail, bonding with nature and stoking her expanding appetite for spirituality.

Feeling thus prepared in soul and body for the rigors of classes and R.A. duties, she began fall semester eager to meet and welcome every student on Wallace third floor. Soon, however, she faced another surprise – a *double* surprise, actually: Christians. Her floor was stocked with believers. The double surprise was that the Christians were, as she describes now, attractive. Loving and open. And somewhat to her dismay, she found that she liked them.

The Conversation

They stayed up late the entire fall, talking about God, faith, history, the Crusades, the Bible, the person of Christ, justice, equality, sexuality, other religions, spirit channeling. She was being challenged as never before. Andrew was the one who made the biggest investment in the Conversation, Andrew from Portland. He was smart, good-looking (as she now says), annoying at times, passionate. He cared about the same causes as she did – women's rights, poverty, racism, but he also cared about ultimate truth. Perhaps most importantly, he *respected* her, the intelligent intuitive-feeler R.A., and sought her well-being above winning an argument.

Sarah resisted the Christians, fought their doctrines. She fell back on her training from childhood when she was able to at least hold her own in the family dinner-table debates, even though just a kid. Nevertheless, the Christians were making headway against her defenses. *And*: loving her along the way . . . she felt it.

"Something started to happen to me over the course of the semester. I can't fully explain it. At first their ideas sounded weird – like, not having sex before marriage. That was crazy talk. My friends and I had mocked Christians who held to that. But in my private moments I was going through a time of profound questioning of my most cherished beliefs."

The investigation

The mental side and the emotional side of Sarah's personality both needed convincing. "As an intellectual committed to finding what's real," she says now, "I decided to investigate the truth claims of Christianity. So I dove headlong into every book on the subject I could find. I read tons of C.S. Lewis, John Stott, Ravi Zacharias and others. I spent January term that year at UC Davis, studying

Christianity, interviewing people, going to Christian events, reading the Bible – including the entire New Testament. And I was so thankful that a professor at Macalester gave his approval for the trip, which was academic in nature but also a personal journey for me. He signed off on my exploration of Christianity as an independent study at UC Davis.

"After all this I had to admit, the case for Christianity was pretty strong. But the feeler in me still needed to experience it, not just analyze it or read about it."

Andrew gave her that chance in the form of an audio tape of black gospel music from his church back in Portland, an unlikely gift to a person who'd spent several years hating on Christianity.

She went out for a run on Summit Avenue, that proud four-mile boulevard alongside Macalester that serves as a joggers' paradise in St. Paul. She plugged in the worship tape, and after a few minutes she realized . . . it was hitting her pretty hard. Or rather, touching her tenderly. Maybe both. "It totally connected with me. I'd never listened to worship music before. I remember running, running so fast . . . I felt like I was flying. The instruments and singing, just the whole experience, filled my soul in such a deep way, like nothing ever before."

Higher Love

Sarah was coming around, hanging a spiritual U-turn from her days as an opponent of the faith. She never expected herself to be sympathetic toward Christians and their beliefs.

"I felt like I was being wooed by a Person, drawn into a different way of seeing things, a different way of living."

Every day she contemplated the foundational shifts in her thinking. God, it seemed, was making himself known to her in smallish ways, dropping little clues in her path. She started up her car four times over a period of weeks, and the song "Higher Love" by Steve Winwood was playing each time. She'd always loved dancing to that song. Odd that an eight-year old musical relic was intruding into her vehicle so persistently:

Think about it, there must be higher love
Down in the heart or hidden in the stars above
Without it, life is a wasted time . . .
Bring me a higher love

"The person I was beginning to pray to but didn't really believe in knew what I needed. God knew exactly what would speak to me at that point in my journey."

Full circle

Thus it came to pass that Sarah Gross converted to Christianity her junior year at Macalester College. It was a gradual process of engaging her intellect and heart, and overcoming an acute skepticism that had resided in her so naturally. She'd always been put off by the hypocrisy of church-goers, until a trusted advisor called her out on how she actually *knew* that to be true. How could she be so sure of her opinion if she wasn't actually involved in a Christian community but only criticized from the outside?

So she joined a church, and of that first experience she remembers, "I found out that while God's people are messy and complicated, the church was also a place of profound love and commitment."

She told her parents the news of her conversion, and they freaked out. Her dad mailed out an article about the Moonies, warning her of the dangers of joining a cult.

But over time they adopted a more supportive role. "They really wanted to be loving toward me and not lose their daughter," she says now with a grin. "The humor of my family was that for Christmas that first year I got three nativity sets, four crosses, a Jimmy Carter book and a Mother Teresa book. So if you ever need me to hook you up with nativity sets . . . "

Quoting the NT

Soon after graduating from Macalester, Sarah joined Catholic Charities as a social worker, and began praying in earnest for her family and friends, that they, too, would find faith in God.

Her prayers were answered quite unexpectedly: Visiting her mom in Washington State, she was hit with a panic attack. "It was embarrassing. I was sobbing, breathing into a bag, and my friend Esther was trying to calm me down. And as I'm having this meltdown, a Bible verse came out of her mouth – *but she didn't know it*. She was in a Wiccan women's circle in those days. She said to me, 'You know this whole faith thing you're exploring . . . I really believe that *all things work together for good, because you love God.*' It just came out of her mouth, a saying from the New Testament [Romans chapter eight].

"After the panic attack was over, I said to Esther, 'Did you know that you quoted a verse from the Bible?!' That incident was actually a turning point for her and she eventually became a Christian."

The vision

In her mid-twenties, Sarah married Andrew – Andrew from Portland – and together they brought three children into the world. The church they currently attend in St. Paul is called Bethel Christian Fellowship (BCF), a charismatic community where the gifts of the Spirit flow freely. Sarah has been given a prophetic ability that enables her to know things and discern things that others may miss.

"Years before I had kids," she says soberly, "God told me that twins were coming. So I prayed for twins. Then a girlfriend of mine got pregnant with twins so I thought, shoot, I was praying for *her*. Then six months later . . . and this was after years of infertility and miscarriage – very painful – I was pregnant with twins."

The most powerful prophetic vision she ever had, however, was just before her fortieth birthday. "I had an open vision of the face of Jesus. It still makes me weepy when I think about it [tears]. I actually saw the face of Jesus. It was just incredible. It happened during a Sunday service, and it was related to the issue of women in leadership in our church. I had two images of the face of Jesus. One was of him weeping over us. The other was of him with his head thrown back, laughing.

"He was showing me that he wasn't angry. My main response to things like injustice – like women disallowed from leadership – is anger. I think what he was showing me is that he was sad, victorious but not angry.

"Subsequently, I became the first woman elder at BCF. I think God was showing me his heart about that. The vision was the most glorious fortieth birthday present you could ever have. I was undone for days – just that sense of being near to the presence of God, of seeing his face."

Healings

She tells of people being healed at BCF, and how in one sense it's no big deal. They don't call the newspapers when someone recovers instantly from chronic back pain or becomes cancer-free after prayer. It's just the "normal" at BCF.

One that wasn't so normal, however, was a dead man come back to life.

"We have a friend from church who was raised from the dead, in India. He attempted suicide and was declared legally dead for several hours. Then the Christian community in India that knew him and loved him prayed that God would revive him, and that's what happened. My kids joke about it . . . 'Yeah, Danny, he was raised from the dead,' then they just wave their hands flippantly like it happens every day," she says, laughing.

"Lots of those things happen here. But I'm also not okay with the wackadoodle off-the-rails crazy stuff which people of my tradition can be guilty of. I think our church has a lovely balance. Our last two pastors have had PhDs. Very intellectual but also Spirit-filled.

Therapist

After marrying Andrew, Sarah shifted from social work to become a licensed counselor and therapist – a successful practice which she maintains to the present.

"We pray for our clients," she says now. "And we see amazing results. People are healed. God gives me insight into their condition that goes way beyond my natural abilities.

"I know that God loves every person who comes to my office. So when I treat people from other faiths or no faith or atheists or whatever, the healing process that we're in is just as holy as someone who professes a faith in Christ.

"That said, there's a kind of wholeness at times that I see, especially in clients who *are* people of faith. On the topic of self-compassion, for example, they begin to pray and open themselves to the things of God. There's a way in which they can connect with having compassion toward themselves, and they can ask hard questions such as, 'God, where were you when I was being molested?' And as the therapist, I don't know the answer. I don't know how God is going to show up in answering their questions, but he usually does. It's incredible to hear the stories of how they begin to hear from him."

Counsel from the counselor

I asked Sarah about this topic of "self-compassion," which is often difficult for people who struggle with guilt and shame, and/or perfectionism.

"I teach and train on this," she replied. "It's basically extending the compassion toward yourself that you would toward someone else. It's not needing to be special or important. It's deep, true compassion toward the self. And from a Christian perspective I think of it as internalizing the voice of Jesus toward ourselves. The voice is kind and loving, though of course we still need to grow and change, but it's from a place of kindness and empathy, not harshness."

To see Sarah now and interact with her is to see a woman full of compassion for herself and others. She seems to possess special insight into the souls of those around her – a kind of "Holy Spirit channeler," you might say.

- 4 -

The Haunting of Deedra Reyess

Rural Arizona

There was a new kind of craziness in the life of Deedra Reyess, definitely not of her own choosing. It had to do with the humming birds hovering in front of her face, the bird feeder swinging in the windless evening air whenever she talked to her dad, the owls swooping and diving around her car, and the coyotes stationed along the road to watch her eerily as her headlights illumined their grim faces, one after another.

Deedra told all this to the *tuhukya*, the Hopi Medicine Man. But somehow he already knew. He also knew about the dreams she'd been having, the visitations from her dead father and the cloak of darkness that had descended on her family's home on the Hopi Reservation. How could he know? She'd said nothing, only that she and her mom were coming in for a cleansing. They'd brought an offering – a pot of beans and some bread.

"The Medicine Man looked at my mom," Deedra recalls. "He said, 'You don't look so good, *Metwi* [a term of endearment]. Your face used to be so bright. But something came over your husband and over your house at Hopi a long time ago. It descended on your home like a dark blanket.'"

To Deedra he said, "That evil thing that's been hovering over your house, well, it took your dad. Some people cursed your family a long time ago. Their intention was to take your dad out, and it finally happened."

In addition to the food offering, Deedra and her mom had brought to the *tuhukya* ground corn meal – considered sacred in the Hopi rituals. The spirit man took the corn meal and stepped outside to pray with it. He came back with something in his hand that flashed with the movement of his wrist – a crystal. He held it up to Deedra's face and peered through it into the depths of her life. "Then he started going over my dreams," she says, "and how my dad was tormenting me. He went over the stuff with the humming birds, because it's not normal for them to come and hover directly in front of you, just a few inches away, and remain there. When my dad was alive we would put food in the feeder for them. And now when I tried to talk with him in my grief, I'd be sitting outside in front of a humming bird feeder and it would start to sway back and forth, even though there was no wind. And when I stopped talking the feeder stopped moving.

"I knew this contact with my dead father wasn't right, because according to Hopi tradition you're supposed to release your deceased loved ones and move on with your life so they can go to their final home and not hang around this world."

A tale of the dead

The Medicine Man continued explaining his diagnosis to Deedra: "You poor thing. How could your dad do this to you?" And he began saying words in Hopi that Deedra only partially understood. "Now I'm going to tell you something about your dad: He made it to the place in his journey toward the final destination. But because he did so many bad things in this life, he has to pay. So he takes only one step per year, and he stands there in pain. So a witch came along and offered to help him reach the other side, and he agreed.

But the dead are not supposed to accept help from anyone. You have to make the journey yourself.

"The witch told your dad that the only way she could help him is if he brought his daughter along. *You.* You're young and haven't done the bad things he did in this world. So the crossing would go quickly for you, and when you arrived at the destination where all the Hopi live, the portal would open for you, and then your dad could slip in with you. That's why he's come back for you. He saw that you were weak, that you weren't letting go of him. So he used you. He wants you with him on the other side."

Deedra suddenly felt like the sacrificial lamb. Her own father would actually want her dead? They'd been so close in this life. Sometimes close in a bad way: when she was doing drugs and booze, he seemed to approve at times, or at least didn't stop her. "He was more of a friend and bro than a true dad," Deedra recalls. "I never had a true dad."

The Medicine Man was just getting warmed up. It was time now to make a decisive break from the dead, cutting off all contact with the nether world. And time to drive away, once and for all, the curse of darkness that had plagued Deedra's family at Hopi. The man told Deedra about a powerful song that can draw spirits out and make them go away.

"So the Medicine Man sat real close to me and sang this song for awhile in Hopi. Then he started working this thing right here [she touches the base of her neck], and he started twisting it. And this thing like a cactus spike came out of my neck, but it was a bone, and he started pulling it out of my skin. And he reached around and did the same thing on the back of my neck. I could feel the bone slide out of my skin. It was the weirdest feeling ever. I don't know how to explain it. He pulled that thing out, and then my spirit was

38

lifted out of my body for a few seconds, and I had this pleasant feeling. Then my spirit slowly sank back down into my body and I went limp on the couch."

Mom and daughter and *tuhukya* then ate traditional bread and spat in a corn husk. The man took the husk outside and did something with it. At that point the portal between dead and living was shut, the ceremony over. Deedra and her mom went home quietly.

What Deedra didn't know then is that there would be unintended consequences as a result of this exorcism. She would be cut off from more than her dad. But maybe that would be a good thing.

Road rages

In the years leading up to this encounter with the Medicine Man, some of Deedra's worst collisions with life happened in vehicles. In seventh grade she and best friend Carrie planned to attend a DJ dance at a neighboring village one evening. But there was no way Deedra's dad was driving them to the event, as he'd promised. He was passed out drunk on the couch. Angry and disappointed, the girls took matters into their own hands, commandeering the family Lumina and driving at age thirteen across the reservation to the dance. They stopped en route to buy a bottle of Captain Morgan Spiced Rum, which they drained together. It was Deedra's first time drunk.

Carrie, the accomplice, ended up in jail. A friend's mom drove the Lumina with Deedra on board back to the thirteen-year old's home and even promised not to rat on her. But a missionary, Brad, bumped into Deedra's mom at the Post Office the next day and asked how the girls were doing.

"Doing?. . . What do you mean? . . . " Deedra's mom had no clue of the girls' escapade.

Oops. Brad wasn't in on the secret, and Deedra was nailed by her mom. But her dad reacted quite differently. When he found out about the girls' car-and-rum adventure he merely advised Deedra to clean out the vehicle and get rid of the evidence. "That's the kind of relationship I had with my dad," Deedra recalls. "Co-dependent, never really healthy.

"And after that, Carrie and I made a vow never to speak with Brad and his wife, Sara – the missionaries – again, because Brad had gotten us in trouble with my mom."

More car incidents, preludes to a grand finale: In high school an abusive boyfriend pushed Deedra out of a moving vehicle, breaking her nose. And later, while living in Phoenix and doing drugs, she got caught going eighty-five in a thirty-five mph construction zone, with the substance ecstasy fresh in her system . . . "Trying to get to the liquor store by two a.m. after a party, that's why I was speeding." That event ended with a DUI and a week in jail.

Things were flying out of control for Deedra in those days. Since earning her high school diploma (barely), she had started receiving "per cap" income – that is, per capita payments from the tribe, generated from casino gaming. She was single, mobile, and flush with cash, a regular "rave" party patron, and deeply immersed in the subculture of cocaine and whatever chic drugs were floating around the Phoenix nightlife scene.

Grand finale

Then the big one happened. Her brother had given her a gun for her twenty-first birthday, "a little 9mm, a police-looking thing," as she describes it. She'd been practicing at the shooting range at Sugarloaf Mountain the day prior, and now the pistol was stashed in the glove compartment of her car, along with a loaded clip. She was on the back roads, headed home from a meeting at Arizona State to her apartment in south Phoenix. "When I was driving along, there was a man in this hooptie looking car, like a gangster dude. . ."

The guy cut in front of Deedra and she hit the brakes, almost ramming him. She threw her hands against the steering wheel in exasperation. The "dude" saw the motion of Deedra's arms in his mirror and mistook the sudden movement for an obscene gesture.

Emotions exploded in both vehicles. The guy moved his car to the side and slowed to match Deedra's pace, flipping her off and yelling profanities, vowing to "get her for this." He had a female in the car with him – his girlfriend, thought Deedra – but the girl just ignored the two combatants and looked the other way. As the cars slowed side by side to a stoplight, Deedra, outraged by the verbal abuse, reached across the front seat, popped open the glove compartment of her car and pulled out the 9mm Glock. She snapped the clip in place, pulled back the top, put a bullet in the chamber and swung the barrel around to aim at the bad guy.

"He just looked at me and froze," she recalls. "I thought to myself, well, I don't want to go to prison. So I could just kill them both and then kill myself, it shouldn't be that hard. I don't have that much to live for anyway. But then I got scared. I think the reality of the situation hit me, the gun in my hand . . . so I dropped the pistol, drove ahead of the guy's car, pulled a U-turn and took off. He got my plate number and reported me. Turns out he was ex-cop, and that wasn't his girlfriend in the car. It was his teenage daughter."

Deedra was facing five to fifteen years for aggravated assault, but miraculously served only nine months. She emerged from prison with a felony on her record, feeling lost and helpless and worthless, and quickly dove back into the familiar world of alcohol and drugs.

41

A left turn

At age twenty-two she took a job as a blackjack dealer. The money was solid and she partied constantly with the dealers and other employees. One night she felt a tap on her shoulder, the signal from the pit boss to move to the next table. But this time it was a summons to call a certain phone number. She had a bad feeling, something to do with her dad, she knew it. She called the number and learned from an aunt that her dad had suffered a heart attack. Deedra asked desperately for the name of the hospital where he'd been taken. She had to go see him immediately. There was a moment's pause on the line and she freaked out. "They didn't take him to the hospital, Deedra. They took him to the morgue," her aunt reported.

There was a funeral for her dad, and the craziness of the animals had started soon after – the flitting humming birds and the swaying bird feeder, owls dive-bombing around her moving vehicle, strange coyotes appearing on the roadside, staring at her as though aware of a pending calamity. The dreams of torment from her father's spirit had begun then as well, leading to the bizarre visit to the *tuhukya*, Hopi Medicine Man, cutting off contact with the deceased and lifting the curse from her family's home, supposedly.

The sum of these events left Deedra shaken, questioning everything, adrift on the highs and lows of the substances she routinely abused. Had she really just been summoned by a dead relative and some animals to let go her earthly existence? To act as a travel guide for spirits in the afterlife? It was too weird. She found herself lacking direction, doubting her own value as a person and, in fact, disillusioned with the Hopi spirituality that allowed for such affliction and even seemed to foster it.

"The Hopi were messing with some powerful stuff," she reflects now, "but it wasn't doing any good. My dad had done the Hopi rituals his whole life, but it wasn't enough to save him. So I checked out. After that I didn't believe in anything. I just wanted to be done with it, to be left alone."

Awakening

Not long after, on a Saturday night, she stayed up late, drinking and smoking weed. Alone. "Sunday morning I woke up early and I just said, 'Man, I've made a mess of my life.' Being drunk the night before, I was tired of feeling like that. I thought, man, I should have my life together by now. I shouldn't be doing this."

That Sunday morning she went for a hike on South Mountain. "I was sitting up there early in the morning. I was thinking about my mom and thinking about Brad and Sara, the missionaries from when I was a kid. And I was like, How do these people have it together? How did my mom, who's a Christian, find strength when all these bad things happened to her? How do they do it? And how do I get from here to that point?

"When I got back to my car I thought, man, how do I go to church? How do I find a church? So I googled churches, and Passages Christian Fellowship came up, and I thought, I don't know . . . maybe I'll just sneak in and sneak out."

She drove to the church and attended the morning service.

"I don't remember what they were talking about, but by the time I got back to my car after the service, I was crying. I felt like God was talking to me, and I felt like I belonged there. I felt safe, and I felt wanted and desired. But I was questioning it.

"Then I went to a ceremony at Hopi. I sat there waiting, and I thought, why am I not feeling anything like I felt in church? How come it's not happening for me?

"So I left, and I was thinking, people that believe in God and believe in Jesus and have him in their lives, they struggle, but they're not like, bad. Compared to Hopi – if tradition really worked, why are people abusing each other, why are they still drinking, smoking weed – if this tradition is really working, then why is it *not* working? How come it wasn't enough to save my dad? I realized I didn't want to be part of that.

"So I went back to Passages the next Sunday. Pastor Keith gave the invitation to make a relationship with Jesus, so I was like, man, I was kind of scared, but I don't have anything left. I have nothing. So I went forward and it was life-changing. It was amazing."

She joined a women's Bible study. "I was the youngest one there for a whole year. But those ladies loved me, poured into me. I grew in my faith."

She got in contact with Brad and Sara, the missionaries. Now laughing as she recalls it, "I told them, 'I have Jesus now.' It had been twelve years. And they said they'd been praying for me this whole time."

Deedra Reyess closed her story to me with these words:

"I have a real Father now. And I've forgiven a lot of the people that hurt me. And most of all I've forgiven myself, especially having this felony on my record. And for me to have Jesus – since I tried meth and slept around and drank alcohol and pulled a gun on people and did all these bad things and treated people wrong – Jesus still made something out of my life. He's still calling me his daughter. I can't fathom his grace, and how loving he is. It's like, 'I love you where you're at, but I love you too much for you to just stay there.'"

Her advice to other young (or old) people who are struggling with despair, anger, loneliness, substance abuse?

"There's nothing you could do to make God not want to love you. You can do a lot of things and create this whole pile of mess, but he has the power to erase it and make you a new creation. There's nothing you could ever do to keep you from his love."

The Curious Case of Cole Foster

Utah

If you were given the following assortment of random items and were asked to build a story around them, how would you put the pieces together? The pieces are: a backyard hammock, an intense rainbow, a pretty Jewish girl, a video game console, a series of one-night stands, Pastafarianism.

Those are the peculiar elements of the life-story of Cole Foster, a cool guy by any measure, and founder of Triangle Fraternity at the University of Utah. When I met Cole and had the chance to interview him, I thought to myself, this guy is going places.

It wasn't always so. He talks about himself as being quite the opposite in high school: an unmotivated cynic who'd drifted off the rails into deep self-absorption. "I pretty much wasted my junior and senior years," he admits now. The outside world a train wreck, his own soul vacant and restless, he distracted himself by pursuing girls at school and the ski slopes of Colorado, and by playing video games.

One other important diversion also took hold of him in high school: Pastafarianism.

"Pastafarianism" is a wordplay on the Jamaican-based religion, Rastafarianism, and a satirical reference to the practice of worshiping the "Flying Spaghetti Monster." Think food (spaghetti) + fictional deity, hence: "Pasta"-farianism, which is meant to mock religion.

An atheist friend had pointed out to Cole how Christians had overstepped their boundaries by imposing the teaching of creationism as recorded in the Bible into the curriculum of certain public schools. This angered Cole so he became a faux follower of Pastafarianism – an act of protest against Christians.

Evolution of a young boy

Many years earlier when he was in elementary school, Cole's parents took him to church. There was a time designated in each worship service when small kids were called forward to gather in a semi-circle around the pastor for a children's story. Cole eagerly joined in and also attended Sunday school for further instruction in the rudiments of the faith.

But he had a different mindset than his fellow grade-schoolers who settled, mostly, for one-way communication. Cole talked back to his teachers. Not in defiance – on the contrary, he was glad to be in church – but simply as a young boy who's curious about God might do: probing the teaching, pondering, trying to make sense of it all, perhaps showing a smallish hint of future skepticism.

For a few years Cole didn't attend church. But in ninth grade he found a compelling new reason to return: girls. They were involved in the high school youth ministry, he was not. For a fourteen year-old boy, a more powerful incentive for religious participation is hard to imagine. "I wanted to go on dates and I wanted to be part of that community, even though by now I had serious doubts about God."

He landed a girlfriend and she took him to Wednesday night student activities at her church. "There was music and it was fun to sing but I never focused my energy toward God. Instead, I was basically singing the songs for her and even *to* her."

The evolution of Cole's spiritual outlook in the years from early elementary school to ninth grade went from "happy church participant" to curious seeker to doubter. Soon he would take another critical step in the process.

It started when he met Jason on a paintball team and they began hanging out, walking around Jason's neighborhood and having long talks about religion and other meaning-of-life questions, and bonding over video games. "Jason helped me explore the possibility of there not being a god," Cole recounts.

Jason told Cole about some inconsistencies he saw in Christianity and the Bible. He also enjoyed ridiculing Christians, and his anger over the teaching of creationism in public schools was very contagious. Cole caught this sense of wrath from Jason, became furious that religion was being imposed on students in school (Whatever happened to the separation of church and state? he thought), and embraced atheism.

The high school atheist

At some point in my interview with Cole I asked him about his emotional state in eleventh and twelfth grade when he identified as an atheist. And while some emergent atheists discover a sense of liberty in finally breaking free from what they see as the shackles of religious dogma and guilt, Cole seemed to go the other way. He lost his sense of direction and purpose. He hung out regularly at Jason's house, playing video games, ditching his homework and not being entirely honest with his parents about his whereabouts. He was a member of the swim and downhill ski teams at school but sloughed off there as well. Any chance for a college scholarship in academics or sports was now off the table.

Cole was also in a cheerless funk. "I became paranoid about what others thought of me. I was always trying to impress – especially girls, and I got discouraged when I couldn't get a girlfriend," he remembers. "I was frustrated with a lot of things such as school and the state of the world around me. I was toying with Pastafarianism but wasn't really exploring any other thoughts. I was very self-absorbed."

He did take up a new sport, however: Make a Christian Squirm. The idea here was to mine the Bible for bizarre passages and use them to pin Christians to the wall. An example is Leviticus 20:9: "Anyone who curses his father or mother shall surely be put to death." Cole would ask a Christian friend, "Do you stand behind a God who commands his people to kill their children if they speak out against their parents?" Then he'd watch them squirm.

Another was the destruction of Sodom and Gomorrah as recorded in Genesis 19, and the fate of the main character's (Lot's) wife, who was turned into a pillar of salt in the process. Cole would press the matter on any Christian who would listen: "Are these acts of God justifiable? Ethical? Do you support this God?"

Bottom line is that Cole was upset with Christianity and moved as far away from it as possible.

Underneath it all, however, was a complicating factor, one that Cole didn't recognize fully at the time. It stemmed from his childhood. It was a light that still shone, though faintly, in the basement of his consciousness. He'd always been a questioning person, daring to challenge the status quo and dominant narrative, which had been Christianity. That's how he'd originally become a skeptic, and now he thought himself as being in a superior position, intellectually. But the internal "complicating factor" was simply this: curiosity.

Like a virus, curiosity messed up everything. It dawned on him that the possibility – even the *probability* – of God's non-existence carried with it the opposite possibility, that maybe God is actually there. But if that were true, which it probably wasn't, God was not within easy reach. Certainly nowhere near the western slopes of Colorado.

A pretty Jewish girl

Cole enrolled at Salt Lake Community College in Taylorsville, Utah, and lived in relational isolation. He'd made no friends in his new city. So he took to reading, which stirred his dormant curiosity but was still a lonely endeavor. He plowed through Ayn Rand's *Atlas Shrugged.* "It was a good story but all I had to do was look at Rand as a person to see that maybe I shouldn't be following her advice about a philosophy of life."

Desiring more human contact and a sense of purpose, Cole joined an engineering society and began volunteering at a local elementary school's Lego robotics league. The combination of reading and human interaction began to have, as he says now, a "thawing effect" on his atheism, and he began to explore various faith traditions.

"I was drawn to how the Buddha had gone on his personal journey. I took brief looks at the Koran and Torah and had conversations with Mormon missionaries, and I began to think that there really is some higher power out there, but nothing specific I could call God. Certainly not a faith of my own."

At age twenty-one, after three years at Salt Lake Community College, Cole transferred to the University of Utah to pursue a degree in engineering. Along with some new friends, he launched a chapter of Triangle Fraternity for architects and engineers, and within a semester they had secured a house on the edge of campus.

They fixed up the place with furniture and a projector, made it feel like home, and lived together in fraternal unity with ten guys.

His social life expanded. He got into a pattern of meeting women at college parties and other venues that resulted in a series of short-lived hookups, aka, one-night stands. "Not a person of good character," he says of himself back then.

Somewhere in the profusion of parties a Jewish girl named Rebecca caught Cole's eye. They talked, hung out for a bit, and Cole's intention was the same as always – "connect" and move on. It was a way of life by now for the rising senior who, just three years prior, had been a certified loner .

In the course of their conversation Rebecca mentioned that she would not have sex before marriage. Normally, this announcement would be an automatic show-stopper for Cole. But not this time. He was intrigued enough with Rebecca to stick around. She was confident, secure in herself. "There was something special there," he remembers. She was involved with faith – and that's what got Cole going to Greek IV.

"Greek InterVarsity" is the sorority and fraternity ministry of InterVarsity Christian Fellowship, a national campus ministry. Rebecca had enough pull on Cole's heart to bring him along, quite happily so, to Greek IV. "At first I went to the meetings and socials just to score brownie points with her," Cole admits. But then things got more interesting. And a little complicated.

The backyard hammock

Rebecca's father is Jewish and when she was twelve years old she celebrated her "coming of age" through a bat mitzvah. Six years later, as a freshman in college, she continued her spiritual journey by embracing Jesus as Savior. The new Christian started a Bible study in her sorority chapter along with another Greek sister – in the face of significant opposition from other members.

Cole was undone by this story. "Rebecca and her friend hung with it," he says passionately, "and led this Bible study all through their college experience. I was so impressed. People didn't want her to do this but she still did what was right. Everything about her, all those characteristics of standing strong, going after what was right – those were the things I was attracted to and wanted for my own life. I was not anything like that."

I asked Cole where they were when Rebecca first made the dramatic declaration (dramatic for him, that is, not for her) of her plans for celibacy. "In my new church," he replied. Come again? "It was in the backyard of our frat house. We had a hammock, green-and-white striped, and Rebecca and I would sit out there on these gorgeous summer evenings talking about God and faith. That's where she first told me she wouldn't have sex. I heard it from her in my backyard church."

Movement

Cole began actively pursuing Christianity. Still entrenched in past habits, however, he did it at first only for Rebecca. But at some point he took ownership of the process for himself. In Greek IV he discovered a welcoming community that allowed him to express his opinions without condemnation. He noticed that opposing viewpoints in the same room of that fellowship didn't turn personal or kill a conversation. He loved that dynamic.

As the summer wore on Cole and Rebecca grew closer. He never dared call her his girlfriend for fear she might reject this title (and him). Nevertheless, a kind of tango seemed to be developing between the two of them, which was freshening by the day.

Then at some point Rebecca dropped another little bomb onto the dance floor: "Cole, I need to tell you, God comes first in this relationship." Any disgraceful, fading hope that remained in Cole's mind of a short-lived tryst with the pretty girl was erased. The old Cole would have done that. But the new Cole – yes, the new Cole . . . What would that person do? What would he be like? Cole himself did not yet know.

The Living Room trail

There's a unique trail that winds up the mountain from the back side of the University of Utah called the "Living Room" – aptly named for its stone configurations of benches and chairs that provide front-row seating for a massive stadium view of the Great Salt Lake and Oquirrh Mountains. In the evening hours around sunset, the Living Room plays host to many guests who ascend the mile-plus trail to witness the entire panorama flooded in horizontal golden light.

It was to this destination that Cole set out early one evening with his new friends from Greek IV, including Rebecca of course, but also a recent acquaintance: Taylor Cushing, the InterVarsity staff member who served as advisor to Greek IV.

Soon Taylor, her husband Zach – whose hobby is photography – and Cole lingered behind the rest of the group on the Living Room trail. And then Zach dropped back even farther to follow his wife and the seeker of God from a discreet distance, camera at the ready. This allowed for a conversation that, as it turned out, was of such magnitude to Cole as to be an epiphany.

Crucial conversation

One of the factors leading to the critical moment in the conversation with Taylor was Cole's reawakened curiosity about spiritual matters finally getting some traction. In Greek IV he found students and staff who were thoughtful about faith and were at least suggesting some possible answers to his many questions.

"I definitely shifted from my previous viewpoint as a critic of faith to an investigator of faith. I saw that it wasn't hurting God to ask questions about him, and that with intellectual rigor I could probe into these matters."

The talk on the trail with Taylor was a major turning point. It centered on the topic of genres of the Bible. No one had explained to Cole before that the Bible is written in a variety of literary genres such as historical narrative, poetry, apocalyptic, law, and prophecy – and that each category is read uniquely, using the same rules of interpretation as in its secular counterpart. You wouldn't read T.S. Eliot's poetry the same as the U.S. Constitution, for example, or the political philosophy of John Locke the same as a biography of Martin Luther King.

"When I had the realization," Cole says, looking back, "that you read Genesis differently than Psalms, for example – that Genesis is a creation story and the Gospel of Mark is a letter and Psalms are songs . . . once Taylor made the point that you read them all differently, I began to see that if I try to pin religious people to things by putting out a literal interpretation of something, and say to them, 'If you support the Bible, then you support this. So why do you support the Bible?' – that was missing the point of what faith and Scripture are all about."

The word epiphany means, among other things, a sudden revelation or insight. That was Cole's experience on the trail. But there is another piece of the story that must be told – or shown. At the moment of Cole's dawning realization about the genres of the Bible, an intense rainbow appeared over the mountain they were hiking – a sign, perhaps, of God's presence and approval of the proceedings below.

Fortunately, Zach swung his camera into action and captured the scene (see back cover for the actual photo). Epiphany thus exploded into theophany on the mountain – a visible manifestation of God. A skeptic might object that the rainbow in question is simply half of a lucky coincidence between a natural phenomenon and a human conversation – two unrelated items. That's one theory, anyway.

Wedding bells

Looking back on his budding relationship with Rebecca, Cole tells me now that she never did give him any sort of ultimatum, as she might have been justified in doing. She never insisted that he adopt faith in Christ or risk losing her for good. "All she had to do was be a loving person," he says, "and introduce me to other loving people who were Christians. That's how I fell in love with Jesus."

Today Cole is a devoted follower of Jesus Christ, though he still has questions, which he probably always will – and he's still against the teaching of creationism in public schools. He works as an engineer in Salt Lake City and volunteers at a youth ministry at a local church. He and Rebecca were married in the summer of 2017.

– 6 –

Una Kim: The Art of Business

Iowa

Una Kim knows well the misery of being crushed and abandoned by a first love, a man whose promises proved worthless to her, his military career serving as cover for a liaison with a lieutenant twenty years his junior. It's why Una stares blankly into space for a short moment when talking of the old days, those days of falling down, emotionally wounded, in the odyssey of emigrating to America from Korea. A mere teenager, she'd come to the U.S. and enrolled at Iowa State to study art, met a guy and married him, and walked the platform two years later in cap and gown pregnant with his child.

She's quite sure now, in hindsight, that even in the first months of marriage he was unfaithful to her, taking undue advantage of her submissive naiveté. She was, after all, learning to trust the people and mores of a peculiar new culture, and that meant extending herself, at some risk, into the hands of professors, administrators . . . and a Caucasian husband.

This husband, she believed, would bring love, security, and inroads to social circles and a career in America. He was a graduate student pursuing a masters in political science, she a mere sophomore undergrad. Trouble had begun soon after their marriage, but she ignored or didn't believe the rumors of his exploits. Or perhaps the young Korean simply could not face another cultural obstacle, one that would, in this case, bring shame down on her head. No, better to let it go, sit back, keep on studying, do the right thing. Always.

She studied diligently for classes – in English, of course, that confounding foreign language. Everything was so impossibly hard, so different here from Seoul. She had come as a shy person, fearful of standing out in a crowd. A trip to a county fair in central Iowa had been a nightmare of stares from local citizens, their curious faces gawking at a genuine Asian "specimen" in their midst – an exotic photo come to life from *National Geographic* magazine. "I felt like a monkey in a cage," she remembers now. "I was lonely; I sobbed through the night so many times."

The immigrant

Born in 1953, she'd come from an affluent family in Korea, her father a self-made man before the tumult of mid-century civil war – North versus South – and the economic desolation that followed. Korea's wealth was gone, spent on the war, so Una left the country in search of opportunity. She flew to the Midwest where a bus from Iowa State University picked her up and carried her to its campus, along with what she hoped was her own internal "success gene" inherited from her lawyer father.

Trouble was, she majored in art – most likely a ticket to scarcity, not money.

But when her husband transferred schools to finish out his political-science work at Indiana University, she also enrolled at the school and made a small course adjustment to her studies that would prove crucial: not art, but *photography*. She'd found her niche, a ticket to potential success.

Rumors of her husband being seen with another woman at Indiana University came drifting on the wind like a tainted odor.

Yet, she thought her marriage was safe, or at least hoped as much. She herself remained faithful, dedicated to spouse and duties and academics, the "ever-steadfast Korean," as she says. Her son was born there in Indiana; surely such a significant event would seal her husband's devotion to the things in life that mattered most – wife and child. But that remained to be seen.

Religion and business

Somewhere off to the side, like a part-time job providing extra stability but little in the way of personal development, was religion. "I was raised in the church," she says, "and my husband was also religious. We attended church on Christmas and Easter but honestly, we didn't have any spiritual life. God was not in the picture at the time. We were just going through the motions."

After a move to Washington, D.C., Una started her own portrait photography business, while her husband continued his grad studies. Their son was two at the time. The family of three had been attending church more regularly but when the business began growing and her free time shrinking, something had to give, so church-going was eliminated. It had been a "ritual thing" anyway, and could always be sought out again, if necessary.

Una found within herself an entrepreneurial drive toward success in business that began to dominate her attention. Sixteen-hour workdays were the norm. She would not be denied, not by husband, and certainly not by any timidity carried forward from the past.

Meanwhile her spouse was moving up the ranks of the Air Force, working at the Pentagon, continuing further studies at Georgetown University, and maintaining yet another guilty *rendezvous* on the side. Una's relentless focus on business blinded her to the truth, however, or at least distracted her to the point of denial. Nor could she afford to lose him now. Business was good, but not that good. Start-ups are notoriously uncertain, unstable, and if she were pared down to just her own shaky income, the immigrant-entrepreneur would likely find herself in serious financial trouble.

The parting

A decade passed, her husband carrying on a double life between home and mistress, she living a double life split between home and her own *liaison* – photography. Looking back, she talks about idols. "When idols came into our lives, there was nothing to resist them. The idol for him was the other woman, for me, business. His girlfriend was a Second Lieutenant, young enough to be his daughter, but he was in love, and that meant there was no going back.

"The way I found out is that my son learned his dad was having an affair, and my husband finally confessed to me, plainly. Back then, for military officers the honor system against relations with co-workers was strong, so had I spoken out against my husband, his career could have been destroyed. He was afraid of what I might say, but I kept it all to myself."

The crumbling marriage was beyond salvage, nothing remaining except the question of whether it would end in civility or acrimony, nice or nasty. The couple decided on the former, and while there were no dogfights on the way to divorce court, Una landed on the other side in a precarious position. The business still had its ups and downs, plus there were payments to make on the house they'd built, a house predicated on two incomes, not one unsteady income. Adding to the drama, of course, she was now a single mom.

"If anything had gone seriously wrong with my business, I would have *nothing*," she recalls. "We'd been married eighteen years, and he walked out on me. I had no security, certainly not my business. I was paying on the house and had just bought a studio as well. I was very worried. I was alone with house and child, the first time I'd been truly on my own, with no family there for me."

Digging in

Looking back, one might justifiably guess that this combination of sad events led to Una's Waterloo, a perfectly understandable defeat. Others in similar despair seek relief in a bottle – or bottles of pills, or a series of sexual encounters, all temporary pain-numbing medications, all eventually making things worse.

Una went the opposite direction. Maybe it was the "success gene" inherited from her father finally emerging. She dove back into her photography career with desperate fury, taking advantage of her own station as a female Korean. "People began coming from Baltimore, Richmond, even other states, because I was an Asian photographer, very rare at the time. I was working long hours during the week and traveling to shoot weddings on the weekends. I had to make my business prosper; there was no alternative, no other source of income.

"Would I do it all over again? The marriage, the house, the studio? Probably not. But I was a courageous woman – foolishly courageous. I don't know what that courage was about. I didn't have the Lord then. It's scary when I think about it."

Immigration, a failed marriage and a thriving business. All by age 40.

A gap

Something was still missing. Hollywood and television tell us the missing piece is a soulmate – Una's now vanished if ever he was truly present – or personal happiness found through family, meaningful work and friends. These solutions are not to be disparaged. Yet, Una was looking for support outside herself, beyond human horizons to a higher realm, and thereby beyond two other Hollywood truisms – that the answers are to be found "within your own heart," if only you are "true to yourself." But she wanted more.

She had driven past Grace Community Church many times, located as it was near Una Kim Photography, so one Sunday, quite simply, she took the plunge. She entered the sanctuary and sat in the back row so as to escape quickly when the service was over. Conducted in her heart language of native Korean, the simple liturgy of hymns, prayers, and sermon had an unexpected affect, gently penetrating the raw sadness and relentless determination that had come to define her. "The hymns – every word sung, I was just crying. Everything made sense. I just sat there sobbing.

"Why did I go there? I knew about the Lord, but I wanted to know him personally. I was craving his presence. I went to church two more times, and I was crying my eyeballs out but also praising God. Probably everyone thought I was a strange woman sitting in the back, who was always bawling but would take off as soon as the service finished. I didn't want to meet anyone."

On the fourth Sunday a woman intercepted the weeping visitor and befriended her. Alone was coming to an end, a new family coming into play, while the visitor's fountain of emotions continued their spillover. "I started praying, asking God to know him better. I wanted a Bible study but hardly knew what that was. I was raised in the church and I knew about Christ, but for me it was not a personal relationship. He was not real in my life. When I met Jesus as a friend I'd been totally alone, so it felt as though he was pouring his love over me."

Things were happening fast. The next week the minister announced they were starting a Bible study, so Una joined. Then she learned about "dawn services" which had no appeal to her as a non-morning person. No matter, she adjusted her routine and made it a daily commitment: church at five a.m. every day. Crazy.

A new love?

Una's son went away to college, and the dream house in D.C., which had held promise of great happiness a long time ago, was now tormenting her with its spacious void – a lonely, empty barn reminding her of a former husband's betrayal. She began praying for a new man in her life, knowing full well that she herself was a new woman, not the fearful schoolgirl who'd grown up so quickly in the Midwest and near the Pentagon in the nation's capital.

The woman reborn was now in constant communication with a God who cared for her and had died on a cross to prove it. In this she trusted, to the core. She laid out a list of requests before the Lord, praying boldly yet humbly. Would God grant her a man to love who didn't put her first, but actually *second* – *behind* his own close relationship with God? This was non-negotiable. She would not date anyone who was not devoted to Jesus, a conviction that emboldened her prayers even more.

A new man, if he was out there and given to her by God, didn't have to be handsome or wealthy, but faithful to her and self-sufficient in his work. She could not, *would* not, carry along a bum who wanted a free ride. He had to love her and also challenge her to grow by contributing something of substance to a marriage. Then she added one final item to the end of her petition, definitely an oddity: "Lord, could he be younger than me? Maybe by five years or so?"

Japanese Garden was a sushi place near her studio, which was near the gym where she worked out several times a week, which was also in the neighborhood of her church. After pushing herself at the gym one day, she popped into the Garden for a spot of sushi on her way to worship, and there was a Navy man sitting at the counter enjoying a meal. A brief, covert reconnaissance of his posture and manner followed: his body angle, kindly face . . . she wasn't certain, and couldn't risk staring. Maybe a candidate for her companionship? Love? She didn't know. Such observations came about in a few short seconds, more felt than reasoned out logically. She had a positive intuition about him, then sensed a powerful urge to *speak* with him, but with an accompanying cautionary alarm in her head. "You simply don't approach men you don't know," she reminded herself, "not these days, not in the big city where good intentions can be misconstrued."

And then suddenly she was approaching him with an uneasy smile and a dash of fear but also the assertive confidence she'd gained in business . . . and prayer. "Hi, you don't know me, but I have a question for you. This may seem weird, but I want to ask if perhaps . . . you are a Christian?"

"Uh?" he said, looking up, surprised. He, too, apparently was aware that women don't normally talk to men who are strangers. "Well . . . yes, as a matter of fact, I am."

"A born-again Christian?" she pressed.

Navy man answered this second question also in the affirmative, and brief introductions followed in which she learned that his name was Steven.

She had to be sure of him. She couldn't afford another mistake with a man.

Later, she agreed to a first date with Steven on one condition: she could give him only one hour on the appointed evening, since she was due at church by seven-thirty p.m. But that plan went out the window as their conversation blew through the sixty-minute mark, well into the evening, knocking out any thought of her running off to church. Nor did she regret the change of plans.

"We've been married nineteen years, and going strong," Una reflects. "God is the center of our relationship, the most important factor in our lives. We end the day with prayers and Scripture."

A word to the wise

Una ended her testimony with a spiritual "exhortation" in Korean, which she translated and is excerpted here:

"Growing up, Buddhism was mixed in with my religion. You meditate, and through meditation you reach somewhere, you empty yourself. But I can tell you, that was no solution. There was no god who would die for me, for my self-centered person. So I came to faith in Jesus and his promise of eternal life. Once I received him, my life was renewed and restored. He has given me hope through his resurrection, and I can't go wrong with that.

"Right now I'm retiring after forty years of having built a successful business. I don't go to dawn services anymore but the first thing I do in the morning is spend an hour in prayer with the Lord. It's a powerful way to start the day. I do have tribulations and trials, like anyone else. But having the Lord to walk with me each day, and every day, twenty-four/seven, it's a different perspective on life.

"And God gave me a wonderful husband. God answered all my prayers, right down to Steven being five years and ten months younger than me. I wish I'd have prayed that he had more money though," she laughs.

"In a castle I'd be happy; in a dungeon I'd be happy. I have joy and peace in God, and I thank him with my whole heart."

York Moore: Death Wish

The slums west of Detroit

The small boom box kicking out the distinctive sounds of Diana Ross was hooked up to a long, black extension cord that ran all the way to the other side of the rundown duplex. York's family was homeless. To survive in a house without utilities they stole electricity from the neighbors, carried in water to flush the toilet, and wrapped themselves in blankets to fight the merciless winter temperatures.

"We were squatters," York recounts now, "occupying a building on Delton Court in an all-white community of mainly poor auto workers, most of whom had migrated to Michigan from Appalachia. Apparently they didn't take kindly to black people moving into their neighborhood, especially if we weren't paying rent. So . . . they sent us a welcome committee."

The ten-year old boy didn't realize the peril of the moment. Suddenly cutting through "Ain't No Mountain High Enough" was the *thud-thud-thud* of objects slamming against the house, windows crashing inward, a clamor of angry voices in the front yard, his parents screaming for everyone to move *immediately* to safety. Confused and scared, he huddled with family members in an interior windowless bathroom, protected from the assault of twenty-five rowdy attackers. Hurling rocks and potatoes at the duplex, they shouted, "Ni_____rs, get out! Move out! You're not welcome here!"

Committee #2

A few weeks later, a local church got word of their situation and showed up with more friendly munitions: clothes and groceries. Again, York was confused. White people the same as before, yes, but no outrage or threats, no potatoes fired at the house but instead, offered as gifts. "They were white southerners," York remembers, "from a nearby Southern Baptist Church. Good folks, well intentioned, but they didn't exactly speak our language or know our story."

Whatever the cultural barriers, York's family soon accepted an invitation to move into the church basement, leaving behind the crappy duplex. The new digs were warm, the electrical outlets and toilets were functional, the hosts were kind, if a little strange. But perhaps the Southern Baptists didn't realize who, exactly, they were taking in.

The family of five consisted of three kids, of whom York was eldest, with highly educated parents – a white father and black mother who were followers of the secular philosopher Ayn Rand. Out front of an earlier home in a different community, they'd posted a small sign that read, "The Moores, Atheists." And they'd kept a barrel out back . . . for burning Bibles.

Thus it was that York and his family, intentional *non*-believers, came to occupy a house of God.

It was a small building with a congregation numbering about a hundred. They invited their basement dwellers to services many times, to no avail. "We felt bad," York says now. "We were eating the food and living in the space, but we weren't attending any of their functions."

Finally, that changed. Several months after moving in, the family ascended the stairs on a Sunday morning to the main floor of the

67

church, where York remembers being greeted by an "enormous, obese white guy. He gathered me into his body and into the entrance of the sanctuary, and I felt so welcome. At the beginning of the service they were singing 'Power in the Blood,' and then a plate was passed around the pews with money in it. I was bewildered. I'd never gone to church before."

Halfway through the service all the kids were dismissed to Sunday School, so he joined about eight other elementary children in an adjacent classroom. The first thing he noticed was the stunning teacher – "a blonde college-age girl with a wonderful physique . . . I'm trying to keep this PG," he says now. "The lesson she taught that morning was about God appearing to Moses in the burning bush, so she asked all the kids, 'What would you say if you saw God in a burning bush?'

"I wasn't shy, so immediately I blurted out, 'Oh my God!' Everyone gasped and looked at me. So I said it again, 'Oh my God!' And this time all the kids grabbed their faces and ears, and the cute teacher's eyes got big, but before she could say anything, I started repeating, 'Oh my God! Oh my God,' over and over. Hey, I was just in fourth grade. I didn't know anything. Finally the teacher yelled at me, 'Stop! Get out! Go back to your parents!'

"So I got kicked out of Sunday School for something called 'blasphemy.' I didn't know what that was. But there was a pattern developing in my life that was very disturbing to me. The pattern was this: I was different, my family was different, our values were different, *and different was not good.* I was not welcome.

"You see, up until fourth grade, I was actually homeschooled, not for religious reasons, not at all. My parents simply didn't believe in public education. They were intellectuals and had master's degrees in the arts, but the state of Michigan was pressuring them to enroll us in public school, so in fourth grade it happened – I entered the system. Believe me when I tell you, that was a dark time in my life."

Darkness

Let the beatings begin. York's mixed racial heritage of white father and black mother gave the outward impression of racial ambiguity. One of his first days at school, as he recalls now with a rueful smile, "I was beat up during recess for being Japanese. And after school, I was beat up for being Arab. I identified with my mother as African American, but no one at school targeted me for that. Other races, yes, but not for actually being black."

Turmoil at home added to York's problems. He didn't know it at the time, but he was stepbrother to *thirty* siblings. "My dad was a serial philanderer and was still married to his first wife (of four in his lifetime) when he took up with my mom. She changed her name for him but they weren't actually married. Finally, everything came to a breaking point. He was buying and selling cocaine, seeing other women on the side, so my mom left him. He was the cause of our family's instability, and when she cut him loose, we moved into a real house."

In middle school York discovered girls and alcohol, made some friends, but was still the target of bullying. "One of my English teachers," he recalls, "returned a test to me with the words, 'You failed, you blankety-blank n____r.' Then the principal recruited some football players to beat me up on my way home from school. Actually, getting beat up started to feel normal to me, like it was just 'Tuesday' or whatever, and not any unusual occurrence. But the constant beatings do something to you. You think people around you always have ulterior motives; your heart gets jaded, you're always on your guard."

York's voice trails off as he remembers the hard times.

The U of M

After a half-decade of low-level discipline and abundant partying, York buckled down his final two years of high school to earn straight A's and set himself up for college. He enrolled at the University of Michigan-Dearborn and dove enthusiastically into his studies. "I loved learning, loved college," he says now.

He had another love that first year as well. Christy. He was certain that she, too, felt the romantic vibe between them – nevertheless, she told him flat-out she wouldn't date him unless . . . unless he became a Christian. But after winter break he came back to school to find Christy dating a Muslim guy. York was stung, once again finding himself on the outside. The old tape played in his head:

I'm different, and different is not good. I'm not welcome here.

He exploded inside and vowed to go on a rampage against Christians – "easy to do," as he says, "because I was a philosophy major. I could write papers against Christians and debate them in class. I also joined a fraternity and my nickname was 'Satan' because I was known as the persecutor of Christians."

Half his reasons for going on the offensive, he admits now, were due to the wounding from Christy, the other half intellectual. He remembers an African American woman who began spring semester quite sure of her faith, but three months later disavowed her beliefs – mostly due to York's tactics in class.

To leap or not to leap?

Junior year, York launched into a philosophy honors project on the topic of existentialism. The big question was whether it was intellectually viable to believe in God as a blind leap in the dark.

70

"But at the end of the paper," he says now, "I came to the conclusion that there are no reasons for God, no real benefits to a blind leap in the dark. Just believing in God because life might be better in the end didn't seem to be enough.

"So I embraced a kind of Nietzschean brand of existentialism – that is, nihilism. Meaninglessness. I remember I turned in this sixty-page honors project to my professor who was also my mentor. I walked into his office and slapped it down on his desk after a year's worth of work. It was a moment of finality. I was about to embrace the *angst* that comes with nihilism, with meaninglessness. I'm at that precipice, I'm at that moment. And as I'm walking back to the car after turning in my paper, I heard this voice in my head, which said, 'If you really believe everything you wrote in that paper, why do anything at all?' I thought maybe the voice was just indigestion or a mental thing, but the question made sense.

"At that point I was a very driven person. I had a fiancée and several girlfriends. I was working, making good money. I was a frat guy. It seemed as if I was on an upward trajectory at a great school, but I didn't have any good reasons for doing any of the things there, any more than I had when I was living on the streets.

"So here I am staring into the abyss of nihilism, and I heard this voice, asking me the question, 'Why do anything at all?' And if I don't have an answer, then the answer by default is: *there is no reason.* And if there is no reason, then why not die? Why not just kill myself? At that time I was living in this horrible fumed, intoxicated, infested, death-ridden place called Inkster. So I thought, hey man, it might just be easier to die. So I made a rational decision that I would consider suicide."

But there was a major barrier to such drastic action for York, call it a barrier of fear. Not fear of dying per se, but fear of what might await the young philosopher on the other side of death, if not (perchance) the nothingness of personal extinction, which is what his rational mind expected.

And yet . . . through classes and studies he'd familiarized himself with various world religions, so he worked through the remaining logical possibilities of his destiny after death: If Buddhism or Hinduism were true, he'd be reincarnated after dying, maybe not the worst of fates. If Islam, he'd go to hell but could work his way back. Allah is merciful. The same with Mormonism, a repository of second chances.

It was Jesus he was worried about. The damn Christians said stupid things like you die once and then face judgment, with the possibility of "eternal separation from God" hanging in the balance like a threatening sword. York remembers: "I thought I better make sure that Jesus isn't the one true God. Because of all these other religious traditions – it didn't matter which one – it's only Jesus that is going to be a problem.

"So I went on this exploration, reading literature. I read the Bhagavad Gita, the Koran, the Bible and several others. And out of all that literature, the Bible was the most confusing – probably because I started with the book of Revelation – 'cause I thought, well, I'll just skip to the end and get the conclusion.

"Then I interviewed a guy I knew, Pastor Loren. I'd gone to his church a few times because the girls were, shall we say, easier there. In his office I asked him, 'How do you know God exists?' He said, 'Well . . . it really doesn't matter if Jesus was born of a virgin or if the Bible is really God's Word . . . How can we know such things?'

"So as a philosopher I thought to myself, Pastor Loren has just thrown out the only authoritative source for his belief system. Anything he says from this point forward is merely personal conjecture. So why should I listen to his opinion any more than the guy on the corner panhandling?"

After several other interviews with Christians, York became convinced: *there certainly is no God.* If Christians had no good reasons for following Jesus beyond personal preference or "just having faith," neither did he. The main obstacle between himself and suicide having thus been cleared way, he decided to go for it.

A fast car

He remembers clearly: "On Christmas Eve, 1989, I decided to take my life. I took my fiancée to see *The Little Mermaid,* and in this old movie theater with four hundred other people I said to myself, 'We're on the verge of a national Christian holiday, in a Christian nation.' And I had this moment of clarity, that it doesn't get any better than this. 'All we're doing, saint and sinner, is entertaining ourselves to death. There is no God, it's just a fantasy. And if that's all there is, I'm going to kill myself.'

"So I dropped my fiancée off, and my plan was to smash my car into a viaduct near my home, right near my favorite mall. I got on the freeway going about ninety mph, but then I began to wonder how the authorities would link my body to who I was, so that my mom could find out. And I'm going through all that in my mind.

"And as I got that strange, twisted courage that it takes to kill yourself, fully *intending* to do so, in that moment . . . a power and a presence outside my own filled the car – filled the car and steered me to safety.

"So I got off the freeway, and I thought, 'That was pretty weird.' I'm covered with sweat, and I'm thinking maybe I'll sleep on it. That was my decision. This was no 'come to Jesus' moment. But I thought, 'Hey, I'll give it a go tomorrow and we'll see what happens then.'

"I know, I'm acting now like it's all cavalier. But at the time I was crying and sweating. It was an emotional experience."

York awoke the next morning, Christmas day, at his mom's house in Inkster. And for the very first time in his life, he prayed. It was a prayer of desperation. He remembers, "Instead of crossing my arms in arrogance, I said, 'God, if that was you last night, I need to know, because I'm still going through with suicide. I'm at the bottom. I have nothing left, and if that was you speaking to me in my car, *tell me*. Please, before it's too late.'"

He went into the living room to join the family gathering. His older brother Eric, home for the holiday, had bought a gift for everyone to enjoy, a large picture frame containing a poem called "Footprints in the Sand." York had seen it before. He'd read it in a church somewhere, maybe at Pastor Loren's, but had dismissed it as Hallmark-style sentimentality. Certainly its message was just shooting blanks against the philosophical prowess of a student from the U of M.

"As I'm reading this poem about God supporting and carrying someone during their 'saddest and lowest times,' the same voice that I heard the night before began speaking to me. It wasn't just an audible voice; it was like a voice that was coming from outside me and inside me at the same time, like super-stereo. It was saturating my being. And I heard God say three things to me. The first two were, 'I do exist.' And, 'I'm the reason you exist.'

"That would be enough for a philosopher. Everything can be derived from those two data points: life, purpose, function, belonging, responsibility, obligation, all of those things. But the third thing changed me forever: 'I'm the one who kept you from killing yourself last night.'"

Crazy the opposite way

York ran from the room in tears, a profound sense of conviction – and relief – in his soul. He prayed for the second time that day, a bit differently this time: "God, if you can take my life and make anything of it, after all I've done against you, I want to live for you."

Many people find their faith in a gradual manner, making headway, then stalling out, finding a nugget of truth, only to fall into doubt. Yet, eventually they get there, ascending incrementally to the top of a spiritual hill.

But not York Moore. The faith he never expected came upon him at a very precise point on his personal timeline. On Christmas eve, 1989, he wasn't a man of faith. By Christmas morning, he was.

If his life was nuts before his conversion, afterward it was nuts in reverse. F-bombs that littered every sentence uttered from his mouth for more than a decade disappeared. Three bouts of drunkenness per week turned to sobriety. He confessed his cheating ways to his fiancée and girlfriends, and he called his frat brothers to tell them the exciting news: Satan had found Jesus!

"Most people didn't take it well," he says. "My conversion was quite a shock to everyone. Ironically, I found myself, once again, different. And different was not good. I have to admit, it was my fault as well. I was pretty off-putting in those days. I went from extreme to extreme.

"I visited my philosophy professor, who was my mentor, at his office. I told him what happened, how I'd come to faith. He looked at me, rubbed his beard like a philosopher would, gazed at the ceiling for a moment, then slammed his fists on the desk and yelled in my face, 'You *prove* to me that God exists!' We never reconciled after that."

York eventually settled down, married a fine woman, and found his way in the faith in a more conventional manner. Yet, he's still pretty radical, which is, I guess, what makes him interesting – and influential. He spends his time traveling the country, speaking at college campuses and churches on what it means to truly follow Jesus, and advocating for women caught in the sex slave trade.

He lives with his family in a lovely home in suburban Detroit, where the utilities all work great. He's written several books, and you can find him and listen to his messages at www.tellthestory.net.

- 8 -

Donald Wellington: Flying High

Japan

Lieutenant Donald Wellington is struggling to maintain altitude and airspeed in the plane, but the weather over the East China Sea isn't cooperating. It's night; he's flying blind, on instruments only, without help from autopilot or radar, engulfed in a torrid, dense thunderstorm. Nor can he adjust altitude, higher or lower, from thirty-nine thousand feet; too much risk of colliding with other traffic. He must stay the course, stay in his slot, hands clenching the yoke (control wheel), his own life and those of four crew members now in the arms of fate or deity or whatever you believe in.

He wonders whether he'll see Tokyo again. Twenty-four years of age is too young to die, especially on a non-combat stage. The mission here is to set up approach aids for ATC (Air Traffic Control) in military bases around the Far East, enabling aircraft to land securely in inclement weather. He'd taken off in Okinawa on a nearly one-thousand mile trip northeast, but now everything was in jeopardy, his Air Force T39 convulsing in seizures, ice collecting on the wings – changing their shape and dangerously affecting required lift, windshield obscured with more ice, his heart and brain screaming for resolution. He throws up a prayer or two to heaven, anything to survive.

According to instruments, Tokyo lies immediately ahead. But to the naked eye the world is a dark muddy fog, the aluminum bird and its crew seemingly suspended inside the turbulent belly of a massive sea monster. *Believe the instruments!* he yells to himself, forcing rational thought to the fore. *Trust your training . . .*

But then the plane breaks into the clear. Donnie imagines an angry beast left behind, its prisoner gone, crew inside the aircraft much relieved. All that remains is a nice soft landing without incident in Japan's capital city. The young pilot lowers the landing gear handle and glances routinely at the panel, seeing two green lights illuminate the cockpit.

But there are supposed to be three. *Three* green lights to indicate landing gear "down and locked."

Another wave of anxiety hits the pilot. What to do, ten miles out from home in a speeding jet with an apparent landing gear malfunction? A horrible bucking, sideways skid down the runway – if you're lucky – is the most likely final scenario.

Options: He can fly past the control tower to ask ATC to visually verify the T39's landing gear as operational, but it's too dark for that, even with the aid of binoculars in the tower. Or maybe just call in the "crash crew" and chance a belly-landing on the runway . . . Or remain airborne until fuel tanks are depleted. All the options stink.

Made aware of the emergency, the plane's mechanic enters the cabin where Donnie is seated, a good old boy from Texas. He'd been down this road before and lived to tell – an engine that died, a tire lost, instruments gone haywire . . . He peers at the panel of three green bulbs, two glowing and one dark. He gently asks the pilot, "Sir, did you check that third bulb? Maybe it's simply burned out . . . "

Donnie lands the T39 on its full complement of wheels, a pair under the nose and one under each wing, the plane taxiing in, now at full stop, crew shaken but unharmed. Prayers answered, it would seem.

Forty-some years later, Donnie reflects on the harrowing flight from Okinawa to Tokyo. "You survive, yes, but not due to your own skill. You're not sure how it happened. That's scary."

World citizen

He'd grown up in Germany and Los Angeles, son of an Air Force pilot who was also an intelligence officer. His dad experienced some close calls in bombers over the years, flying missions during World War II and on into the 1960s.

A military family on the move, the Wellingtons lived in West Berlin up until Donnie's second grade in school, then transferred to Los Angeles to embrace the Dodgers, the Beach Boys, surfing . . . "I was vaguely familiar with the idea of faith," he remembers of those days. "American culture was theistic at the time. Most teachers would require kids to recite the Lord's Prayer and the Pledge of Allegiance. But we didn't go to church."

From Los Angeles back to West Germany in sixth grade, Donnie was a Boy Scout and soccer kid, with no spiritual interest. He'd seen Billy Graham on TV in the U.S., so he knew of the famous evangelist, and now there would be a "crusade" taking place in Berlin, the summer of 1966.

Covert kid

The thirteen-year old military boy hops a bus with a non-denominational "youth chapel" organization to attend the big event at the Deutschland Halle. Speaking through an interpreter, Mr. Graham surveys the audience of eleven-thousand Germans and internationals, challenging them to "Turn back to the God of your fathers" and "Set a moral and spiritual tone for the rest of the world."

An invitation is given for people to come forward and "receive Christ" as their Savior. Donnie feels convicted and is ready to join the multitudes migrating to the stage area to speak with counselors, but a warning bell sounds in his head. He thinks of the first rule of military intelligence on foreign soil: *no public identification*. If you see someone you know around town, even your father or mother, act like you don't know them. West Berlin is so small, you have to play by the rules, have to "blend into the woodwork."

The boy resists the impulse to march down to the front. Too much exposure, he thinks, the spotlight too glaring. Surely Christ was not confined to the platform, and would meet him here in the seventy-first row of the Deutschland Halle. "I had no doubt I was making a lifetime commitment to the Lord that night," he says looking back.

Except that's not what happened. Not at all.

After the crusade Donnie quickly forgot about Christ, focusing instead, as he now says, on "myself as the number one priority. I became very selfish and also very indifferent toward God. God moved further away from my windscreen [windshield of an airplane]."

West Point

Passing through boarding school back in the States, Donnie was accepted at West Point and recalls a brush with religion there: "We had mandatory chapel at West Point. When Sunday morning came around, it was a twenty minute march, in formation, up the hill to the chapel; then we were dismissed afterward, one company at a time, and marched all the way back to brunch. It was an annoying obligation that killed half of every Sunday and made no positive difference in my life. I was pretty much asleep, spiritually."

Test pilot

He graduated West Point at age twenty-one and dove immediately into pilot training. It began in Arizona, but soon he was stationed in Tokyo where the T39 flight from hell took place, then transferred to Europe. He flew in England, Turkey, Spain, France, establishing ATC protocols at twenty different bases.

Then as a Forward Air Controller, he piloted a Cessna 0-2 Sky Master, a "spotter plane," twin prop, which marked targets by depositing specially made small rockets on ground positions, so the big fighter-bombers coming up behind knew where to drop their payload. More training maneuvers, not live combat.

It was all good, but Donnie had his mind fixed on a different kind of flying. Fighters.

Top gun

He got his wish at Nellis Air Force Base in Las Vegas, and now was living the dream – fighter pilot in his early thirties, loving his job which consisted of flying subsonic A-37 jets for good pay, driving a sports car around town, "unmarried and unencumbered," he remembers. "I was the epitome . . . the cliché of a single captain on flying status."

Naturally, he was adrift in secular culture, thinking little of things beyond his own pleasure.

Except this: there was a philosopher of sorts striving to emerge from within. Donald Wellington was a thinker, a trainer, even a tactician at heart, not merely a playboy pilot roaming the bars and casinos of Sin City. Perhaps it was these deeper instincts that created within him openness to an unlikely possibility, one that began in a seedy shopping center, downtown Las Vegas, 1984.

Kids and a lion

This wasn't the famous "strip," glamour district of the desert city, but rather the middle of town in a rundown bookstore, its shelves overflowing with detective fiction, romance novels, travel memoirs, and back issues of *Life* magazine.

Donnie was browsing for a leisurely read when he came upon *The Lion, the Witch and the Wardrobe*, C. S. Lewis's first book in the *Chronicles of Narnia* series. Donnie'd never heard of the book or the series, didn't know of their existence, but he paid seventy-five cents for the privilege of owning a copy of *The Lion . . .* , carried it home, and mowed it down in a single day.

Lewis's characters seemed to jump from their pages and yell into the slumbering soul of the soldier. He was stunned, awakened by the allegory, a man accustomed to Mach-speed danger brought to his knees by a group of fictional English children, thrust as they are in the tales into a fantasy land ruled by a wicked witch.

The children's voices find natural amplification in the ferocious roar of Aslan the lion . . . Aslan, noble Sovereign of Narnia, sacrificial lamb of redemption, warrior-servant, battling the witch in shockingly antiheroic ways. Donnie drank of the story eagerly, a man parched and thirsty for realities beyond himself.

He returned the following morning to the bookstore, acquiring the second volume, *Prince Caspian*. He devoured it in twenty-four hours, a pattern repeated seven times to the very end of Lewis's climactic story, *The Last Battle*.

As the tales unfolded through a week of intense reading, Donnie felt himself tumbling down through a fantastical portal into the world of Narnia. Dwarves, dragons, and talking animals, children valiant but flawed, the forces of good versus overwhelming evil, the loving oversight of Aslan . . . "I was stunned," Donnie recalls. "Everything hit me; it was all so compelling. I re-learned the gospel through allegory."

But being a Christian hadn't occurred to the military man in almost two decades, career and self-gratification dominating all else. Spirituality, what was left of it, had been ignored, buried, shut away in deep hibernation.

Record shop

Stirred by his encounter with *Narnia*, Donnie found himself increasingly aware of the divine, as though heaven were reaching down to awaken a soul long neglected. Not that he had been looking for any such connection, here in single pilot's paradise. Or had he?

Then, another unexpected contact with transcendence: Tower Records.

He enters the famous record store off West Sahara Avenue in Las Vegas, a shop known for its vast selection of music, to browse the aisles for LPs and tapes. He notices, up front, a sales guy behind the counter sporting tattoos, piercings, leather – pretty radical for the day, definitely an implicit claim to "music industry insider," quite avant-garde.

But something is amiss in the shop. The overhead speakers normally blasting forth the pulsating strains of Jimi Hendrix, The Who or The Talking Heads are playing songs from another world, songs from Amy Grant.

Amy Grant? Christian pop singer serenading Tower Records – not possible! Donnie feels his heart jolt as he looks again toward the front counter, at tattoo guy, who calmly meets his gaze. Could it be, this is all . . . *deliberate?*

The soldier turns back to the record bins, riffling absently through massive inventory, pulling each cardboard LP jacket forward as though in a file drawer. Dionne Warwick, David Bowie, Hall and Oats . . . he doesn't see the names, his mind undone at the oddity of the moment, but also pried open to receive a Nashville girl's simple melodic call:

Guess I've known it all day long
Wonder where my thoughts went wrong
When will my heart believe?

Any second now, Donnie thinks, The Spinners or Blondie will break in, displacing Amy Grant. The Tower playlist will return to normal, he will get on with his career, a strange side-trip to other-worldly dimensions will end. He presses fingertips into his forehead, straining to figure things out, finally pleading silently, "*No . . . no, don't return to normal, not back to ordinary.*" He really wants extraordinary.

And in all the earth there is nothing worth
Half as much as life with You.
'Cause the people and the things we're counting on here
Are gonna' pass away too

Decades later, he says of himself back then, "I knew it. You can run and hide, but you're only hiding from yourself, can only distract yourself for so long. But God was still there. Amy Grant being played in Tower Records, that cannot happen. That was the voice of God, saying, 'I'm still here.'"

Leave it all behind you
Love has found you now

Iraq

At age thirty-three Donnie was assigned to an inspection team that traveled around the country evaluating pilots' flying skills on "check rides," and examining their flight records. He was in Pittsburgh, carrying out assessments, when he got a call that someone of his skill-set was needed in the country of Iraq, *pronto*.

Serving as Air Attaché in the American Embassy in Baghdad, he coordinated airlifts with other attachés that brought in U.N. peacekeepers, much needed in the protracted Iran-Iraq war that was beginning to wind down after eight years of fighting.

Dinners and receptions at other foreign embassies – French, Japanese, Chinese, British – contributed to gruelingly long workdays, followed by required viewing of Iraqi television news, just to stay abreast of the war.

After hours, he delved into a stack of albums and cassettes left behind by an American who'd vacated embassy living quarters before Donnie moved in. Among the treasures in possession: Van Morrison's album, *A Sense of Wonder*, its first song on the A-side entitled, "Tore Down a La Rimbaud," followed by "Ancient of Days."

The ironies pile onto themselves as Donnie found revelation in Morrison's compositions, the first song based on the French poet Arthur Rimbaud, who'd vehemently rejected Christianity, depicting himself as "urinating" skyward in defiance of the Creator.

85

Morrison had been inspired by Rimbaud into self-exploration, the fourth line of "Tore Down a La Rimbaud" reading, "gave me knowledge of myself," and later in the song, "showed me light out of the tunnel." The lyric doesn't say who'd done that, but Donnie connects the dots back to God.

Another lyric in Morrison's song was most profound of all to the pilot: "Showed me pictures in the gallery" reminds him of a statue of Christ's head he'd seen in Rome, created by Bernini. And "Showed me novels on the shelf" brought to mind again the *Narnia* series he'd recently read.

"Ancient of Days" seemed to Donnie more explicit about God, though Morrison denies attachment to specific creeds. Nevertheless, the singer portrays the Ancient of Days (a name for God in the Bible) "shining in the sun this morning . . . standing by the winding river . . . shining in the starry night," and even "stirring in my heart this morning."

Maybe it was the juxtaposition of Morrison's thoughtful musical expression with Donnie's immediate environment of a senseless war, a half-million soldiers lost in eight years of butchery.

"Van Morrison's album had a major influence on me," Donnie remembers, "putting me more in touch with God. It seems as though God was always poking in, making his presence known.

"I never had a radical change in my life, more of a slow dawning. I came to faith in Jesus very gradually. I began to see the difference in how I interacted with people. My life wasn't just about my career and pleasure anymore, but about serving country and people around me in the name of Christ."

Pentagon

After the war, Donnie moved to Alabama to be a writer for the Air Force, and married a woman named Gail. He was recruited into a war planning shop of the Pentagon, one day before Saddam Hussein invaded Kuwait in 1990, so he and Gail moved, necessarily, to Virginia.

Promoted to Lieutenant Colonel at the Pentagon, he served as a strategist for "Desert Storm" and other operations, his main job that of creating basic doctrine – foundational ideas for using air force in wartime, both generically and in that particular Middle Eastern theater.

On 9/11 he was out of town speaking at a conference. From a hotel room he was horrified to watch reports on television of terrorist attacks on the Twin Towers and Pentagon, thankful to be alive while mourning his injured and dead colleagues back in D.C.

Today, Donald Wellington works at the Pentagon for the Vice Chief of Staff, his steady hand and critical mind giving guidance to the massive chess board of USAF maneuvering around the globe.

Donnie's advice

His counsel to others, whether military or civilian:

"God is always with you, always will be. The better you get at recognizing his presence in all circumstances, the more joy you will have."

And of his own story he observes, "The Lord was faithful. He pursued me despite all my neglect of him. I didn't know what would open my eyes and my heart, but the Lord certainly did."

Not bad for a guy who found Jesus Christ, ever so slowly and indirectly, through children's fiction, an "out of place" Christian pop singer, and a mystical, Northern Irish R&B rocker named Morrison in Baghdad.

- 9 -

Nicole Chong:
Swing Dancing with Jesus

Los Angeles

The Chinese American girl from Covina, California, is new at UCLA. It's "Zero Week" – the week before classes start – when freshmen are supposed to mingle with each other and get into the groove at college. Nicole forces herself outside the safe confines of her dorm room in Hedrick Hall, attempting to make friends. Naturally shy, it takes a huge effort.

Descending five flights to the first-floor, she musters courage enough to enter the main lounge. A card game is going on – poker, she soon learns. Several students are deep into the game but they greet her kindly and invite her to join the action. She declines without hesitation. Not a card player. Yet, she remains close at hand, hoping to connect, hoping to find companionship at this mammoth university.

Glancing casually around the walls of the lounge, she spots a poster inviting students to go "swing dancing." She's never heard of swing dancing, doesn't know what it is, but somehow it sounds appealing. Maybe it has something to do with jazz, one of her loves. She makes an off-hand remark to the group which, oddly enough, affects the rest of her life: "Swing dancing sounds like a lot of fun."

The zealot

Her statement had been an innocent utterance, like commenting on the weather. But not to Brandon, one of the poker players. Brandon is obsessed with swing dancing and would walk barefoot on shards of glass to convince anyone to try it.

He leaps from his chair up into Nicole's grill: "Oh my gosh, dude, you should go! Swing is so awesome." He grins at the newcomer. For him, this is too good to be true: a ready-made dance prospect practically landing in his lap.

He drops his cards, pulls Nicole over to the side and starts demonstrating a few dance moves. Sure, the two of them had only just met, but this is urgent business. She protests, "I can't dance. I don't want to go. I was just kidding . . . it was a mistake! Forgive me."

But the zealot does not give up. "After that," she remembers, "every single Tuesday I managed to run into Brandon. I felt so unlucky. He would ask the question, 'Are you coming to swing?' and I would always make an excuse. But I felt bad turning him down so many times."

By the ninth week of fall semester Nicole has some solid friendships in place, mostly in the dorm, Brandon among them. He stops by her room on a Tuesday (of course) with his usual query: "Hey Nicole, you coming to swing?" She shakes her head no, a little embarrassed.

The challenge

Another friend she'd met earlier in the semester, Luis, is with Brandon. Luis decides to intercede, asking her gently why she never goes to swing. She replies that she's scared and has two left feet and can't dance and would be really bad at it. He pokes at her playfully, "It might actually be fun for you, Nicole."

She shoots right back, "But what if it's *not?*"

Then, more soberly, Luis presses a point that alters the course of her life: "You got to take a risk. If you never take risks, you'll never know what's good. How do you know if swing's fun or not unless you try it?"

He was right, she always plays it safe. She prefers the known to the unknown, security to adventure, familiar to the peculiar. She hates the thought of going to swing but finally, after so many weeks of standing strong against these guys, she acquiesces: "Okay, let's do this thing."

The trio marches off to swing dance, Brandon's face glowing with satisfaction.

Arriving at Sunset Rec Hall, second floor, the room is small, stuffy, filled with twenty students. She takes a swing lesson, rotates around the circle so that she dances with everyone who's there, and loves it. By the end of the evening she's hooked, sold on "swing" after just one session. She never misses a Tuesday dance the rest of the school year. Bonus: Brandon isn't bugging her about it anymore.

Christians

She had learned along the way that many of her new friends in the dorm are Christians. The second week of school they'd knocked on everyone's door on the floor, inviting them to dinner. She herself had hesitated, but finally said yes. Nervous the entire meal, her face was rose-red and she felt awkward making conversation with people she didn't know.

That was her first event with InterVarsity Christian Fellowship, the name of the campus ministry to which the Hedrick crew belonged. Thankfully, she'd made it through dinner with them unscathed (mostly).

A Christmas "party"

There were more meals, more hangouts, then that pivotal ninth week when she'd finally gone swing dancing, solidifying many friendships.

Her new friends began inviting her to InterVarsity events, but she didn't like this because it meant more occasions to automatically refuse. She was always saying no to something, which bothered her. So when a Christmas party invite came her way, she thought, what could be the harm in a Christmas party?

The Christmas party: She enters an off-campus apartment and suddenly feels apprehensive, wondering what she's gotten into. Her friend Allen ("Allen from Redding") is her only security. She trusts him but hopes desperately he doesn't leave her alone in a corner to wither away. Sweaty hands, crimson face, feeling self-conscious, she's stuck in this place with no graceful way out.

The party-goers sing spiritual songs she doesn't know, they talk about a Bible passage she doesn't understand. She doesn't know what to say or think, but Allen stands with her. He is kind and reassures her – *Nicole, you're doing fine.* She's not so sure.

She decides in the end this wasn't a real party after all, but rather a religious celebration. An *unparty* party.

Questions surfacing

After the unparty, the diffident freshman vowed to herself she'd never attend another InterVarsity event.

Until, that is, Allen invited her to the next event. It was called "Discover Catalyst," designed for students who were not

Christians. Allen told her straight-up that it was meant for people like herself who were not believers, to learn about Jesus in a non-threatening setting.

"I don't know why," she recalls, "But I said yes. I remember that day so clearly because I was really nervous, my face was really red."

Catalyst: The twenty-five minute hike across campus to the Discover Catalyst calms her nerves a bit. Arriving at Rolfe Hall, she finds a big crowd mingling outside the meeting room, talking and laughing, some taking photos in front of a large InterVarsity poster. She is greeted multiple times.

Music emanates from the meeting room and seems to beckon, drawing her through the doorway. She thinks to herself that this bash, whatever it really is, crushes the Christmas unparty, hands down.

Inside, she notices at the front of the room strings of lights framing a prominent stage area, and on the stage a band playing, Luis himself being one of the singers. He'd be proud of her, she knows, for taking the risk to come here. They're playing popular songs from the radio, no religious music. Everyone is enjoying themselves and she is feeling strangely at ease.

The evening speaker, Shayla, gives a short talk about finding God in her life after walking through some hard times. Afterward Nicole cannot remember her main point but she's suddenly aware of spiritual questions bubbling to the surface of her consciousness. Nor can she get over the fact that so many people around her believe in a god they cannot see, hear or touch. How do they do it? She cannot understand.

The spirituality of her own family consists of a cultural mix of Buddhism and Confucianism, hanging mostly in the background, practiced only during occasional visits to her grandparents' gravesite when prayers are offered to her family's ancestors. Otherwise, religion is absent. Nicole has no active belief in anything beyond the world of the here-and-now.

The conversation begins

She pounds Allen with questions on the half-hour journey back to Hedrick Hall from the Discover event. Why does God allow so many bad things to happen in the world? What does God think about LBGTQ? How can you believe in something you can't see? At the dorm they dialogue for an additional two hours.

She recalls, "I thought, wow, it's so interesting how they think. I was curious about how people can believe in God, but then it hit me: Could *I* also believe? That was the first time I actually thought about it."

Can This Wait?

Next up on the calendar is Winter Conference on Catalina Island, called "Can This Wait?," which serves as the follow-up to the Discover Catalyst.

Allen comes over and knocks on Nicole's door, breaks out a flyer and reminds her of their recent conversation when she had so many questions. The conference, he suggests, would be the perfect time and place to work out some answers.

No way, she's not going. She didn't sign up for all this. Yes, these Christians are her friends and the discussions are good but that's as far as it goes. She tells her pal Allen no, flat out. He says okay but asks her to at least think about it, and they'll talk later.

Just before the deadline to sign up, she's in Allen's room to deliver her final answer: "Allen, I don't think I'll be attending 'Can This Wait?.' I'm just not interested."

He replies, "Nicole, have you ever been to *Catalina Island?*"

She pauses. Her heart jumps. "OMG, I've never been to Catalina
. . . But I've always really wanted to go . . . "

A few days later she and Allen are on board the Catalina Express,
departing from the dock at Long Beach, for the hour-long ferry ride
to the big island. She's excited to experience the ocean-view vistas,
the premier hiking and kayaking, and the sheer mystique of Catalina.

Hearing God?

Friday evening at Can This Wait? everyone is gathered into a big
meeting room for an ice-breaker. She hates ice-breakers.

A speaker named Josh then talks about a story in the New
Testament where Jesus turns water into wine to help a Jewish family
save face at a wedding they're hosting. "Jesus is *generous,*" Josh
observes. "He gives you so much more than you are expecting."

She considers this statement. Jesus actually sounds like a cool guy,
but she's not sure she even believes in him.

Then Josh asks everyone to pray. Pray? She doesn't know how.
She's never prayed. The instructions given, however, are not about
talking *to* God but about *listening* to him: listen to see what word of
affirmation God might have for the friend sitting next to you – in
her case, Allen.

She closes her eyes and strains to hear the voice of God, tries
really hard for about two minutes: *God, if you're actually there, give me
something. Say something. I want to hear you speak.* But she hears nothing,
no "still, small voice" as it's sometimes called, no divine prompts,
not anything at all. Just vacant air. She feels disappointed, defeated.
She opens her eyes in frustration and addresses Allen: "Sorry, I
didn't get anything from God for you." A fresh little wound seems
to open somewhere inside her.

After the session, students scatter in pairs to process the evening. She and Allen go out to a majestic cliff overlooking the ocean, and he asks her, "Nicole, where are you at with God?"

Everything slows down. A little light goes on in her head. She says hesitantly, "I think . . . I'm open. Like . . . if there *is* a God, I think I'm open to knowing him. But . . . if he's out there, I want a sign." Just hearing herself utter those words, she recognizes – *wow, I guess I'm actually open to this.*

It was an unexpected realization for the non-practicing Buddhist-Confucianist, quasi-atheist UCLA freshman.

The last night

On Saturday, recreation at Catalina really kicks in. Nicole plays hoops, goes on a lovely hike, feasts her eyes on the ocean of teal-blue rippled glass that surrounds the island. Then it's back to the business of Jesus. The evening speaker, Gina, invites everyone to accept Jesus into their lives and enter the "kingdom of God."

But Nicole is not ready. Apparently . . . It *Can* Wait. This thing called "kingdom of God" is too far out there for her, too much of an unknown. She declines the invitation but thinks maybe she's letting Allen down, who no doubt had high hopes for her faith to blossom this weekend. After the meeting she looks over at him questioningly, but he says everything's cool; and it seems to Nicole that he really means that.

The GIG

Back on campus, Nicole cannot help but ponder the wind of change blowing softly through her soul. She wants to learn more about Jesus. This is odd because not long ago she knew little of him, nor was it a concern of hers. Somehow Jesus had come flying into her life out of nowhere.

Or maybe he had been waiting for her all along on some mystical dance floor.

She begins attending InterVarsity's "Catalyst" meetings Thursday evenings, where three hundred students gather for worship and teaching. She enjoys this weekly event but still feels out of sorts during the prayers. And every time a call to faith is made, she grabs the sides of her chair, talks herself out of it: *Is this the day for faith, Nicole? No, not today. Maybe next time . . .*

Meanwhile, she begins studying the Bible with Allen and Brandon. They pick out passages and help her understand them, most of which are about Jesus. But the passage that hits her hardest is actually from Psalm 139, written a thousand years before the time of Christ:

"You created my inmost being; you knit me together in my mother's womb. I praise you because I am fearfully and wonderfully made."

This text penetrates Nicole's remaining defenses. She recalls, "It reminded me that even though I didn't have many of the qualities I admired in other people, God made me this way, and I should be happy with who I am. I think of God holding us in his hand, kind of like a doll, just putting little pieces on us, just slowly taking his time. That passage really affected me because I had a lot of self-confidence issues back then."

On the fence

Summer comes and she continues to ask questions of her Christian friends. By the fall, now a sophomore, she decides she must make a decision one way or the other. Either she believes in God or not, is in or out.

She learns that InterVarsity's fall conference is being held at Catalina Island, so she signs up eagerly.

Saturday night on the island the meeting turns, unexpectedly, into a healing service. The speaker declares, "If you are a son or daughter of Jesus and you would like to be healed right now, would you please stand up."

This is crunch time for the Chinese American woman. Should she stand or not? Does she count as a daughter of Jesus? She hasn't yet made the decision to follow him with her life. Most everyone around her stands, because they all need healing for something, whether physical or emotional.

And for seemingly the thousandth time, Nicole remains seated, declining yet another invitation.

Healing prayer goes on for a half hour, and she's feeling weird. Something's wrong. She has a sense of being excluded, left out in the cold. She's jealous of all the students who are talking to God and receiving healing (for sprains, tendonitis, trauma, etc.), but she's not one of them.

In small group afterward, she's processing her emotions, and it finally hits her. She recalls, "I thought about it, and hmm, if I'm feeling jealous, then that means I want something that I don't have. And what don't I have that all these people have? Then in my head it clicked, *I want Jesus.* It just clicked at that moment."

She raises her hand and tells her group, "I have something to say." Five faces look at her expectantly. "I think I want to accept Jesus." She starts crying and the other members pour out their own tears to comingle with hers.

They pray for her and at that moment Nicole Chong takes a huge risk. She ventures onto a spiritual dance floor that seems to have been prepared for her long ago, perhaps in her mother's womb, as Psalm 139 had depicted. She accepts the outstretched hand of Jesus and they start to maneuver through a series of turns and twirls. She sees in his eyes the reflections of three caring, persistent friends – Brandon, Luis and Allen. They are the rascals who set her up for this. It dawns on her in that moment that she's somehow swing dancing with Jesus, strange though that may sound.

Nicole's parting thoughts

In my interview of Nicole at UCLA, I asked her a concluding question: What would you say to someone who's seeking God but is afraid to take that final decisive step of faith?

"Take a risk. I'm so glad Luis was willing to say that to me. I needed to hear it. I knew I had to do this for myself. I had to become a follower of Jesus, and I'm so glad I did. I've found true happiness. So yeah, take a risk. Step onto the dance floor and see what happens."

- 10 -

Rick Mattson: Lost Rocker

Small town America: Marshall, Minnesota

At age fourteen, when I was a bundle of explosive hormones packed inside a skinny kid's body, I joined the Confirmation class at Wesley United Methodist Church. I'd like to say I was there for the religious education, but to be honest my reasons for participation were more earth-bound, their names being Darla Schultz and Amy Johnson.

Confirmation is a rite of passage in the church were you learn the basics of religion, perform acts of service, and eventually get "confirmed" in the faith of your baptism. But I didn't have much faith at the time – aside, perhaps, from a vague belief in a Creator who got the universe started, somehow.

Attending the classes never got my faith off the ground. It was tough to engage with subject matter such as John Wesley's theology of sanctification with Darla and Amy seated so elegantly in front of me, dominating my line of sight and attention.

Perhaps I would come alive, faith-wise, at the upcoming graduation service? It was a ceremony scheduled for the end of the year when all confirmands would go before the church to make our vows and be received into the full fellowship of believers.

It's a day I'm unlikely to forget.

Calamity

Graduation service, as it turned out, fell on a scorching hot Sunday in June, and unfortunately our church hadn't yet invested in air conditioning. The other confirmands and I were dressed in stuffy, constricting Confirmation robes, angelic white, with a collar that rode high and scratched the neck. We were seated in the front pews of the sanctuary, squirming in the heat, when Rev. Halverson called us forward to kneel at the altar to affirm our faith in God and service to the church.

We all made it to the altar, but soon the oven-like temperature hit us hard, and the fallout began. My pal Bruce was first to leave his post, pulling away from the wooden railing to sit backwards at the altar, head in his hands, facing the congregation. He couldn't take the sweltering conditions. Mary slumped forward but managed to use the railing to hold herself up. And then I saw a flash of white to my left and heard a commotion as Ronald hit the floor. I never did like Ronald so I can't say I was sad to see him go down.

Heroically, my utmost concern was for the health and safety of Amy and Darla. I imagined myself carrying them down the middle of the sanctuary with everyone watching in admiration, out the back exit, where I would perhaps administer a new thing I'd heard about called mouth-to-mouth resuscitation, all in the line of duty.

It's well known that fainting, like yawning, has the power of suggestion in it. As more kids slumped over, conscious or not, and adults rushed forward to assist, I could feel my head getting loopy, the annoying white robe smothering my body increasingly every second. So I stood and backed up, shakily, toward the front pew without ever turning around, till my backside hit wood. I plopped down and watched the remaining calamity and recovery efforts from a safe distance.

That's the moment my faith was truly confirmed. Confirmed, that is, as *inactive*.

An objection

Now some might object that there's really no such thing as an inactive faith. You either have it or you don't. I beg to differ. My thinking went along these lines: *Sure, I believe in some vague notion of God, but nothing that would tie me down. Life is about maximizing my own pleasure and achievements. The God I'm learning about here at church is boring and irrelevant and is* NOT *going to help me reach those goals.*

And yet: *If pressed to the wall . . . yeah, I suppose . . . Okay, God is there, but I plan to be different than everyone else when it comes to religion. I'm going to have it both ways – faith and no faith. Faith is the backup plan in case anything goes drastically wrong. But the main plan is to rely on my own determination and efforts for the fulfillment of my own desires, girls being the main object in view.*

The stage

My two younger brothers and I grew up on the stage. Dad was a music teacher so my parents had the idea when we were in grade school to put us in front of local townsfolk to sing songs from movies such as *Mary Poppins* and *The Sound of Music,* and eventually from bands such as The Beatles, The Carpenters, America, Elton John, and others.

The Mattson's family band expanded its reach from local Golden Age Club meetings and Crazy Daze appearances to supper clubs, corporate parties, and showrooms in night clubs. We landed hard-to-get gigs in Madison, South Dakota (population 4,900), Des Moines, Iowa, and other glamour spots.

And then in 1975-76 we spent extended time traveling the country in an attempt to hit the bigtime, à la The Jackson Five, Osmond Brothers, and the fictitious Partridge Family band. All major success stories of the day. It was quite a risk for my parents – and I admire them for it – pulling three teenagers out of school to go on the road in search of fame. I had a great time.

I remember that year sitting on a barstool in Amarillo, Texas, between music sets, talking with a local businessman. He asked what I did in my spare time. "Golf by day, guitar by night. That's my whole life right now," I replied.

"A girlfriend somewhere?" he asked.

"Yeah, back home. Lisa's her name. She's cool."

"But in the meantime, you're out here on the road." He was egging me on.

"Yeah, well, I've met a few girls," I admitted. "I can't really say I've been completely faithful to Lisa . . ."

And so it went, me striving to construct a life of pleasure and success but hitting some roadblocks – such as my own questionable morals and, especially, the American public not falling down in adulation of our band. Actually, we did well. But there were no Disney contracts, no bookings at Caesar's Palace, no TV deals.

We came home in May of 1976, pretty polished in our presentation, to the Ramada Inn of Marshall, for two weeks of shows. Many of the locals were eager to see The Mattsons after our tour around the country, and I was certainly eager to impress.

Bright lights

I never told Lisa about my various trysts in the cities we had traveled, so she came out faithfully to the Ramada showroom to

103

hear my brothers and me play tunes for the locals and for whatever room-renting guests that might drop in.

The house was packed most of those two weeks, never more than on Saturday night, May 22, 1976. I felt an intimate connection with the crowd that evening. Everything we played seemed to be a home run, ratcheting the room higher by the minute as we toured through thematic medleys of Elvis Presley, The Eagles, Johnny Cash, America, and others too distant now to recall.

The dance floor was stomping and packed with bodies, alcohol flowing abundantly, hands groping in places my mom told me not to notice, which of course I didn't. But I did notice my fingers flying fast all night, fueled by adrenaline, zooming up and down the neck of the ebony Les Paul guitar that rested so naturally against my body.

The final songs at midnight were special renditions of two hit selections from the pop group, The Fifth Dimension – "Age of Aquarius" and "Let the Sun Shine In." If it were somehow possible, the hordes of booze-aided party-goers rose to even loftier states of euphoria as we boys played out the final choruses, emotion exploding from our instruments and throats. We hit the last chord with a prolonged rumble that lasted a melodramatic thirty seconds, ending in a synchronized jump into the air, and – *boom*! . . . the concluding note pounded with finality.

Applause and cheers followed. Bows from the three brothers. Mom watching from behind the spotlight, Dad on the stage with us at his keyboard, smiling with satisfaction; Craig the drummer, behind me on the platform, high-fiving with a friend. Lisa pushed forward through the mob to give a celebratory hug. I was in a paradise of my own making – faith, whatever it was, definitely not needed.

Change of pace

Then suddenly I was adrift. The curtain fell on the showroom, the crowd dissipated, the world grew terribly quiet. I guess for a few days I fooled myself into thinking that *celebrity* would be a way of life for me going forward. But to my shock and dismay, the good people of southwestern Minnesota had lives to live that didn't include endless fandom of the Mattson brothers. My smallish star was fading, an inconceivable outcome to my fantastical imaginings of destiny and greatness.

Lisa moved on from me to greener pastures, no doubt a wise move for her. She was leaving an empty shell of a guy who cared only for himself and for whatever pleasure he could derive from those around.

I fell back to a stalwart friend, Dave Musser, my childhood golfing pal, to lift me from the doldrums. I must have been miserable company, but Dave took it all in stride, my foul mouth and base desires standing in contrast to him – a guy who never cussed or ran others down behind their back, and never cheated in golf or on his girlfriend. That's a lot more than I could say for myself.

We indulged a few days of golf at the Marshall Country Club, re-living our childhood. And then Dave took compassion on me – or maybe it was pity – and seeing an opportunity when I was depressed, invited me to a church service.

Not the invitation I was expecting. I'd have gone to an Edgar Winter concert or a golf tournament or a party to meet girls. But not to church. We were on the final hole at the club, Dave beating me as usual. I didn't know what to think.

"Rick, I know you'd like it. It's an outdoor event with a picnic, over in Balaton, at the Skandia Free Church."

Three other friends would be there as well, including Dave's girlfriend – the ultra-talented Tammy Tillemans – and my long-time neighbor, Sam Galbraith. They'd all be speaking and/or singing in the service.

Believe me when I tell you I had nothing else on the calendar that Wednesday night in August of 1976. Absolutely nothing. Yet, I was hesitant. This sounded like some kind of a cult meeting.

But I couldn't deny the fine qualities that were evident in Dave and his company of friends. These folks were overflowing with love and joy, I with sarcasm and despair.

I agreed to go.

Skandia

The setting for the service at Skandia was outdoors on a warm, overcast evening. Minnesota can be gorgeous in the summer, and this was it. I remember my neighbor Sam stood up and talked about being in the light . . . walking in the light . . . darkness had no power over the light. A laser beam shot into my shrunken heart when he uttered those words. The idea of hope and a different way of life began to dawn on me.

Then Tammy sang the old Andrae Crouch hymn, "My Tribute." The lyrical inflections of her voice, the graceful posture of her body – her manner could not have been more incongruent with the performance techniques required in my own world of showmanship. She seemed caught up in a reality beyond herself.

At the end of the service I departed with a gigantic question mark over my head regarding the direction of my life.

We went back to another church, this one in Marshall where we all lived, and I met Pastor Arnold Conrad, who told me right away to just call him Arnie . . . Arnie?

When I heard him preach it was different than anything I'd heard before. His words had authority. I'm not saying he himself had any special authority beyond his position as a pastor. Rather, he seemed to be a conduit of an authority he could barely contain. This made me want to refer to him as the Most Highly Reverend Conrad, ever more. But Arnie it was.

From the pulpit his call to the congregation was to follow the teachings of Jesus and to embrace Jesus in personal faith. I'd never heard this before either, perhaps because the gospel message wasn't preached that way in the religious services of my boyhood, or I wasn't listening. More likely the latter, as I think back to Darla and Amy. But now I was listening. Intently. In fact, not only listening, I was *hearing*. There's a big difference.

Personal revolution

I held out for awhile, kept God at arm's length and even maintained a small separation between myself and the Christian friends I was running with. It was all pride. I still wanted to find my niche as a rock icon and girl magnet, but I was slowly coming to reality. Slowly coming down to the humble level of a Savior born in a stable, rejected by his people, murdered for claiming to be the Son of God, sacrificed for my sins.

This all became real to me over a period of months, and in October of 1976 I went over to Dave's place with my other friend Randy, who'd also been sharing the message of Christ with me, and I announced simply to the guys, "It's time. I'm finally ready."

We sat on the living room floor and prayed together. I was getting used to the idea of praying aloud, something I never did as a boy. I prayed my prayer of "accepting" Jesus, then plunged out the front door into the starry night, filled with wonder at the God who created it all and was offering me life and hope.

That evening was my true Confirmation. It was a decision to stay at the altar and profess allegiance to God, and not let a little fainting spell or a force ten times more powerful – girls – stand in the way.

I met up with Lisa a few months afterward to share the news of my awakened, active faith. She saw in me quite a different guy than before, and she knew right away that her former boyfriend, in his own strength, was incapable of such change. Not even close.

A few weeks after this meeting, she too committed her life fully to Christ.

Lisa and I went on a campaign of sharing the news of Jesus. We told Kelly, Laura, Alex, Craig the drummer from our band, Johnny, Doug, my brother Randy, Bill and a few others. They all eventually came to faith, their lives changed, like mine, from a focus on self to a focus on God and others.

Not that we became perfect saints. Far from it. But we were all amazed to see the power of God transform our lives, and that is true to the present day.

Epilogue

I wrote this book for one simple reason: to be an encouragement to you. It seems to me that those who actually find faith love it, and those who love it share it. This is my way of sharing it. And what better way than this? – to enlist nine other people to share their stories alongside mine.

Perhaps the best way to process what you're learning from the stories is to spend some time using the Reflection Guide on page 110.

And if you think you may be ready to place your faith in Christ – whether "again" or for the first time, please see pages 112-13. There you'll find a simple prayer of faith commitment.

Lastly, please think of another person with whom you can share *Faith Unexpected*. Then, pass it on!

To order additional copies for friends, co-workers, church visitors, employees, please see:

www.faithunexpectedstories.com ($10 paperback) or online bookstores ($12 paperback, $5.99 ebook).

Reflection Guide

I.   The book as a whole

Which stories did you relate to most, and why?

Describe your feelings when you read those stories.

Is there anything there than can inspire your own journey?

II.   Each story

Write out (or discuss with a friend) your thoughts and feelings after reading this story. Did anything here inspire you? Give you hope? Make you upset? What questions did you have?

More specifically, what was the presenting problem or tension point for this person? That is, what drove them to find a spiritual solution?

What was the nature of this person's faith? Was it mainly intellectual or experiential, or a combination? Describe yourself in these terms. Are you mainly a thinker or a feeler, or both?

III. Next steps

If you are interested in awakening your own faith or finding a new faith, write down some action steps you can take, such as reading the New Testament in the Bible (I suggest starting with the Gospel of Mark), visiting a church, talking with a Christian friend, or reading a great author such as C.S. Lewis.

How to Solidify Your Faith

Perhaps you're a person with a "dormant" or inactive faith, and you'd like that to change. That's how I was, growing up in Minnesota. See my story that begins on page 100 to learn how my faith was awakened and came alive.

Or maybe you've never had a faith you could call your own, and you'd like *that* to change. That's the story of York Moore, which begins on page 66 and takes some unexpected turns.

It all begins with acknowledging that you've been created by God to be his son or daughter but have neglected, ignored, or rejected God. For many of us, this is the hard part – admitting our flaws, admitting we're a sinner. But it's the only way to truly find peace with God.

Secondly, you believe that God sent his Son, Jesus Christ, to pay for your sins by dying on a cross and rising from the dead. This is what we call the "Good News"! It means salvation is a *free gift*. God did something for us that we cannot do ourselves, no matter how hard we try. The idea of a free gift can also be difficult for us. We think we need to earn our salvation, but that's not how it works.

Thirdly, you accept Christ into your life and trust him with all that you are and have. Fourthly, you connect with a Christian friend who can help you grow in your faith. So go ahead and pray the prayer on the next page, then tell a Christian friend about your decision.

Sinner's Prayer*

Dear God,

I know I'm a sinner, and I ask for your forgiveness.

I believe Jesus Christ is Your Son.

I believe that He died for my sin and that you raised Him to life.

I want to trust Him as my Savior and follow Him as Lord, from this day forward.

Guide my life and help me to do your will.

I pray this in the name of Jesus. Amen.

*from www.peacewithgod.net and the Billy Graham Evangelistic Association.

About the Author, Rick Mattson

I work as an "apologist" for InterVarsity Christian Fellowship. That means I travel around the country to college campuses making a case for the Christian faith.

Often my presentations take the form of an event called "Stump the Chump," where students can ask the Chump (me) any question they wish about Christianity. My job is to offer a thoughtful reply.

In churches, I help lay people and pastors work through the hard questions of faith, like why bad things happen to good people, how to think about the relationship of Christianity to other religions, and how to have productive conversations with atheists and other skeptics.

I make my home in St. Paul, Minnesota. I'm a committed family man (and serious golfer!).

Prior book: *Faith Is Like Skydiving: And Other Memorable Images For Dialogue With Seekers And Skeptics* (available from InterVarsity Press and online retailers).

Blog and website: www.rickmattsonoutreach.com

To order more copies of *Faith Unexpected,* go to:

www.faithunexpectedstories.com ($10 paperback) or online bookstores ($12 paperback, $5.99 ebook).